Praise for *They Called Me Renée*

'*They Called Me Renée* is an incredible story of an ordinary young woman who survived an extraordinary period of history. A story of how identity changed for the purpose of survival can alter the person you were born to be, giving you the courage and resilience to become not only a survivor, but someone who goes on to make a difference in their community and their world in general . . . The pacing and personal voice of Ruth makes for a gripping, focused story where the stakes are high. If you loved *The Nightingale*, you will love *They Called Me Renée*. A wonderful true story which I believe will still be read generations from now, by all ages, cultures, and genders.'

Heather Morris, author of *The Tattooist of Auschwitz*

'A slim volume of great power. This part memoir, part tribute is beautifully written and deeply affecting.'

Clare Mulley, author of *Agent Zo*,
shortlisted for the Women's Prize

'A masterclass in resilience. This extraordinary memoir captures the breathless terror of occupied France and the fierce, unyielding courage of a young woman who refused to be broken. This is a luminous portrait of survival and a powerful reminder of the light that can be found in humanity's darkest hours.'

Ellie Midwood, author of *The Girl Who Escaped from Auschwitz*

'Extraordinary. Heart-rending. Inspirational. A gripping chronicle of true courage, heroism and resistance, in the face of ultimate evil. A triumph.'

Damien Lewis, author of *Zero Six Bravo*

'An extraordinary true story of courageous survival and fearless resistance against the Nazis. Beautifully written.'

Robert Verkaik, author of *The Traitor of Colditz*

'Ruth Uzarad's first-hand account of her journey from a young sheltered daughter of modest shopkeepers in Berlin into the resistance fighter known as Renée Sorell is a gripping and heartbreaking account of courage and coming-of-age. In honest and authentic prose she shares her gripping story. Glimpses into the future, when an older Ruth returns to the old sites, visits with her long lost friends, fellow refugee children and resistance fighters, and rediscovers her past, lends this account a profound layer of compassion and understanding.'

Gwen Strauss, author of *The Nine*

'What makes *They Called Me Renée* so moving is the sense of before and after. A lovingly described domestic world is shattered the day in 1938 when the Nazis come to the house to arrest the author's father and he disappears forever-from one day to the next everything is lost. Survival depends upon strategy and luck. The eighteen-year-old Uzrad makes the terrifying journey from Berlin to Lyon where she joins the French Resistance. She does not think of herself as heroic. This is what you do. You fight back.'

Rosemary Sullivan, author of *The Betrayal of Anne Frank*

'Unforgettable. A rare coming-of-age story of a young Jewish teenager who fled Nazi Germany and joined the French resistance. 'Renée' survived unbelievable hardship and risked all to save the lives of countless Jewish children. Her deeply moving memoir is a powerful testament to human resilience and survival. A must-read!'

Claire Hubbard-Hall, author of *Her Secret Service: The Forgotten Women of British Intelligence*

They Called Me Renée

They Called Me Renée

The Incredible True Story of a Young WW2 Resistance Fighter in Her Own Words

Ruth Uzrad

monoray

First published in Great Britain in 2026 by Monoray, an imprint of
Octopus Publishing Group Ltd
Carmelite House
50 Victoria Embankment
London EC4Y 0DZ
www.octopusbooks.co.uk

An Hachette UK Company
www.hachette.co.uk

The authorized representative in the EEA is Hachette Ireland,
8 Castlecourt Centre, Dublin 15, D15 XTP3, Ireland (email: info@hbgi.ie)

Published in Israel by Valcal Software Ltd, 3 Rothschild Blvd
Tel Aviv, Israel 6688106

Distributed in the US by Hachette Book Group
1290 Avenue of the Americas, 4th and 5th Floors
New York, NY 10104

Distributed in Canada by Canadian Manda Group
664 Annette St., Toronto, Ontario, Canada M6S 2C8

Hardback ISBN: 9781800964389
Trade paperback ISBN: 9781800964396
eISBN: 9781800964402

A CIP catalogue record for this book is available from the British Library.

Typeset in 13/18.5pt Adobe Garamond Pro by Six Red Marbles UK, Thetford, Norfolk

Printed and bound in Great Britain.

10 9 8 7 6 5 4 3 2 1

This FSC® label means that materials used for the product have been responsibly sourced.

FSC
www.fsc.org
MIX
Paper | Supporting responsible forestry
FSC® C104740

This monoray book was crafted and published by Mala Sanghera-Warren, Emily Campbell, Chris Stone, Mel Four, and Sarah Parry.

In memory of my beloved father, who died in the concentration camp, Bergen Belsen

My courageous mother, who bravely left her daughters behind in order to save them

My husband, David (Dadi) Uzrad who without his help, support, determination and dedication, this book would not have been written

Special thanks to my sisters, Betty and Bronia

Remember the past
Live in the present
Trust the future

Dedicated to Abba Kovner,
the founder of the
Museum of Jewish People
(Beit Hatfutsot)

CONTENTS

INTRODUCTION

"Grandma, were you in the Holocaust?" my twelve-year-old granddaughter asked me one day.

The question confused me and, for some strange reason, angered me.

In a typically Jewish manner, I replied with a question. "What do you mean, was I in the Holocaust? Do you mean to ask if I was in a death camp? Fortunately, I wasn't. I wasn't in a death camp." And with that, I closed the subject.

Several weeks later, in a discussion over coffee and cake, my daughter-in-law asked, "Why did you stay in Nazi Germany?"

Now, as well, I replied with a question. "Do you think it was so simple for a family with children to just up and leave everything—possessions, an apartment, our livelihood? Do you think other countries in the world hurried to open their borders to receive Jewish refugees persecuted by the Nazis?"

Again, it wasn't the place and time to expand on this subject.

But I was asked similar questions, and on the few occasions that I was forthcoming, I noticed the subject inspired interest, which motivated me to try and write down what I'd been through during those years.

I'm not the only one. Thousands of Jewish girls like me wandered through Europe and tried to survive. It's very hard to dredge from the recesses of memory events that happened more than fifty years ago—without the aid of diaries, letters, and documents. I tried to tell my story without adding or detracting, without embellishing or deleting. Perhaps my friends, who made part of the journey with me and experienced the same events, remember something else.

This book is dedicated to my four precious sons, my beloved daughters-in-law, and my lovely grandchildren, who give me such happiness. They were born here, and for them, the State of Israel is a given.

Ruth, Betty and Bronia, undated.

A FAMILY PORTRAIT IN BERLIN

My father, Josef, called Yosel by the family, was born in Dukla, a small Polish town in the Carpathian Mountains next to what is now the Polish-Slovakian border. He didn't talk much about his childhood. He was the youngest son from his father's second marriage. During World War I, he was drafted into the army of Emperor Franz Josef, and when the Austro-Hungarian Empire collapsed, he went, alone, to Germany. My father was short of stature, with a pleasant face that wasn't typically Jewish. He had beautiful brown eyes and high cheekbones. When I read about the Khazars on the Crimea peninsula who converted to Judaism, I imagined my father as a descendant of those people.

My father was very meticulous about his clothes. When he left the house, he wore a hat and a tailored three-piece suit made of high-quality English wool and took his walking stick. He was so meticulous that he made my mother miserable; every speck of dust on the furniture, every little scratch, bothered him. Before he was drafted into the army, he studied in a yeshiva and was fluent in Hebrew and Aramaic. He wrote German using gothic script, but didn't master the syntax of the language.

My father was an observant Jew who embraced religion with all his heart. Every morning, he put on phylacteries, shaved with a special ointment, and washed his hands, and he prayed before every meal. He would say to me, "When all the Jews of the world observe the *Shabbat*, the Messiah will come."

His words confused me. I couldn't understand why all the Jews couldn't observe the holy *Shabbat* at least once.

My father admired Germany greatly for its order, cleanliness, and precision. I remember we received postcards in the mail from Poland, and my father said, "You see, Ruth, here's the Polish mail seal. You can't discern a thing. Look at the German mail seal—everything is clear. The date, the hour, the place. That's Germany for you!"

***

My mother was born in Korczyna, a town not far from my father's birthplace. She lost her mother when she was thirteen. My grandmother died from the typhus epidemic that plagued the town during World War I. Mother had to leave school to look after her two-year-old twin siblings and take care of the house. She wasn't sad to leave, as the Polish girls bullied her because she was Jewish.

When the war ended, her father—my grandfather—decided to follow his son Marcus and move to Germany. My uncle

Marcus was my mother's older brother. In the dead of night, my grandfather, my mother, and her young siblings, Max and Betty, stole across the Polish-German border. The family settled in Berlin, in Grenadier Strasse, right in the heart of a neighborhood inhabited mainly by Jewish immigrants from Poland. The Jewish way of life was maintained in the poor neighborhood, and my grandfather found work as a teacher in one of the many religious centers (*beit midrash*) there.

I assume that my parents met and married as a result of a *shiduch*, as was common in their circles. My mother, an attractive maiden, was twenty-two when she married, and my father was five years older. The wedding took place in the well-known Czech resort town of Carlsbad. The rabbi they found there made sure, for a fair penny, that the young couple received an official marriage certificate.

***

I was born in 1925, a year after my parents' wedding. My mother continued managing my grandfather's home, and we all lived in a two-room apartment on the fourth floor, beneath the roof. My grandfather slept in the kitchen. Next to him, on a folding bed, slept my uncle Max. The living room included a big dining table, a bookcase, and a sofa, on which my aunt Betty slept. Next to the living room was my parents' room, which faced the street. In the room was a huge double bed as well as my bed.

Although our living accommodations were crowded, I enjoyed a warm, loving, lively home. My uncle and aunt, Max and Betty, were eleven years older than me. Max would take me for rides on his bicycle, take me to the cinema, and spoil me with sticky candies. Betty and her friends played with me and included me in their board games. At the age of four, I already knew how to recognize German poets and authors—Goethe, Schiller, Lessing, and others. I would sit on Grandfather's lap, and he would teach me the Hebrew alphabet.

Papa left early and came home late. I did not want to fall asleep before he came home, but my eyes would close before he returned.

The area, Grenadier Strasse, was lively with store after store and *beit midrash* after *beit midrash.* I remember a store for books and religious flyers that was situated next to a fish store with a big pool of live carp. I remember a bakery that gave off enticing smells of fresh caraway bread and poppy rolls. I also remember the cackle of chickens in a cage and righteous women who would check if the chickens were fat enough for the *Shabbat* soup. In all that tumult, one could hear the voices of the students from the *beit midrash* as well as those of the older Jews who devoted themselves to study. During *Sukkoth*, quick hands built decorated *sukkahs* in the yards of the houses, in which boys and men ate. My mother would walk down four stories, carrying pots of food to bring to the *sukkah.* I innocently asked her why she and I were not part of the holiday feast.

When I was five, my sister was born. Her name was also Betty, like our aunt's name. By then, my parents had left Grenadier Strasse and rented a spacious apartment in the building where my father's shop was situated. We lived on the first floor, just above the shop. My life had changed very much—from a pampered only child, I became a big sister with responsibilities. We left the atmosphere of an extended family and lived as a nuclear family—a father, a mother, and two daughters. We moved from a bustling, dirty area to a quiet neighborhood with beautiful parks, avenues lined with chestnut trees, and tidy playgrounds. From a neighborhood that was populated mainly by Jews who emigrated from Poland to an area of mainly Christian Germans.

Our apartment had three very large rooms and a small room for the maid. My parents' room and the "good room" overlooked the street. The children's room, the bathroom, the kitchen, and the maid's tiny room overlooked the yard. In the long corridor leading from the entrance and separating the bedrooms there was an exercise apparatus that combined a swing, rings, and a pole, courtesy of my uncle Max. On Saturdays, holidays, Sundays, and when we had guests, we ate in the "good room." During the rest of the week, the room stood empty. In the summer days, we spent many hours on the balcony, and during warm summer evenings, we ate our dinner there.

Mother helped Father in the shop, and our live-in maid was in charge of the housework and took care of us. She was a young country girl who loved to take us to the park, play ball and hide-and-seek, jump rope, and play games with other children. It wasn't long before I started speaking with the special Berliner dialect. Our maid sang us ballads about unrequited love and thieves with hearts of gold and many more songs with multiple stanzas and refrains. She also took me to church for the first time in my life. She told me about her success with her many suitors when she went dancing on Sundays. All this drew me closer to a new, unfamiliar world.

Our new environment also influenced my mother. Geraniums and petunias bloomed on our balcony, as on our neighbors'. On weekdays, we ate potatoes with herring or potato patties with applesauce, and for dessert, chocolate pudding with vanilla sauce. Instead of the bagels and onion rolls that we consumed when we lived on Grenadier Strasse, we ate simple black bread. The gentiles' food.

On Thursdays, my mother would travel to Grenadier Strasse to buy supplies for *Shabbat*. It was a long, tedious journey, and she would return in the evening, her baskets bulging with carp, kosher chicken, fresh *challah*, and products one could buy only there. Toward the end of the week, the wood floors were waxed and the doorknobs, cutlery, and large silver candlestick were polished until they gleamed. On the large stove fueled by coal stood pots with fish, chicken soup, and more. A fresh yeast cake emitted enticing smells. When evening fell, the long table was covered with a spotless starched white tablecloth, and on it rested two *challah* breads sprinkled with poppy seeds and covered with a gold-embroidered serviette. A silver goblet for the *kiddush* stood at the head of the table, before my father's place. I would arrive at the *Kabbalat Shabbat* bathed and wearing a festive dress.

Friday evening was also my mother's finest hour. Her head covered with a scarf, she would raise her arms and make a circle with them, as though she wanted to embrace the entire room. Then, she would cover her face and present her pleas and wishes to God. Sometimes her prayers would continue for quite a while. By the time she finished lighting the candles, her face would be glowing. She would bless us with a "*Gut Shabbes,*" to which we would respond "*Gut Shabbes, Mutti.*"

Papa would bless the wine and let the entire family drink from the goblet. Then, he'd break the *challah*, dip each piece in salt, and we'd say "*Hamotzi lechem min ha'aretz.*" Only then would we sit down, and Mother would hurry to the kitchen to bring the meal. The menu for Friday night never changed; we started with cooked fish, continued with chicken soup with thin noodles, then broiled chicken with carrots, and for dessert, applesauce or plum and dried apple compote. After the meal, Papa would sing and tell us stories of the sages of the Torah and Mishna.

On Saturday morning, Papa would go to the nearby synagogue, which was an hour's walk from our home. Sometimes I'd accompany him. Papa would walk quickly, while I almost ran to keep up with him. During the prayers, I would stand next to him and he would translate them into German. In the first rows sat the dignitaries, wearing top hats and fancy suits. They had tiny prayer shawls, while Papa had a huge one that covered all of him. While they read the Torah, the children played in the synagogue yard.

I especially loved the *Shabbat*'s long hours of dusk, until the first stars appeared in the sky. The entire house was shrouded in caressing, calming gloom. When the *Shabbat* was over, Papa would say "*Hamavdil,*" while I held the braided *Havdala* candle and my sister Betty held the silver perfume box. After the *brachot*, Papa would pour a bit of wine on the plate and put out the candle, and as he sang "*Shavua Tov,*" the *Shabbat* would end. The magic was over.

Sunday also had a special feel. Like the gentiles, we'd go to Grunewald, a forest of pines by the city. We would pick red berries and wildflowers. We would sometimes enter a café, and Papa would order bubbly drinks in various colors. Once in a while, we would board a tour boat that sailed the beautiful lakes. After our excursion to the forest, we would enjoy Mother's excellent sandwiches. Sundays were also for visits at the famous Berlin Zoo or beautiful Botanical Garden. There, in the greenhouses, Papa would point at the lemon and almond trees and proudly say, "In *Eretz Israel*, trees like this grow outside, not trapped in greenhouses."

Sometimes we would visit Uncle Marcus, who lived with his family in a prestigious area in West Berlin. Our visitors consisted mainly of my aunt, Papa's sister, and her three children. But the truth is that we didn't get many visitors. Maybe it was because of the distance, and maybe it was because of my father's introverted nature. He hated small talk.

***

On an overcast day, in March 1931, it was my first day of school. Mother accompanied me, just as excited as I was. On my back, I carried a black rucksack of tough leather and, in it, a wooden pencil case with pencils and colorful chalks, notebooks, and a book. On my shoulder, strapped diagonally, was a bag containing an aluminum box with sandwiches for mid-morning.

The school was a gray, gloomy, threatening place. In the long corridor, my mother said her goodbyes, and I found myself alone in a classroom with forty girls. They were thin, with fair skin, and I stood out with my curly black hair and plump body. The teacher's name was Ms. Lebrecht, which meant "straight and narrow." She looked the part too—dry, her clothes lacking color and grace, and her silvery hair pulled back severely. During our first lesson, we learned to sit quietly. Not just quietly, but in complete silence, so much so that you could hear a pin drop. At the end of the day, Mother waited outside for me. In her hands, she held a surprise: a bag shaped like an upside-down clown's hat, almost as big as me, full of sweets.

It wasn't long before I learned to read German, and by my second year at school, Papa decided it was time for me to learn the holy language. So twice a week I went to Hebrew lessons. It was then that I became familiar with the Bible stories that the rabbi told us. I especially liked the story about Joseph the dreamer and the story about wise Abraham, who knew the idols were worthless and broke them. Compared to those, I found the stories of the Nibelungen—about the adventures of Siegfried and the god Wotan, which I studied at school—frightening and repulsive with their cruelty.

Müller Strasse, where we lived, started in the heart of Berlin, in a bustling commercial area, and crossed the Wedding quarter, which was populated mainly with downtrodden and unemployed workers. Before Hitler rose to power, the area served as a stronghold of the Communist party and was called "Red Wedding." There were four- and five-story buildings there, built around neglected yards, without trees or greenery. Stray cats searched the garbage cans for food, and the staircases reeked of the heavy stench of cabbage cooked in pork fat. Men, both young and old, gathered aimlessly around the entrances to the buildings wearing tattered jackets without any shirts beneath and smoking cigarettes that they rolled themselves. Young girls or women who passed by were subjected to whistles and crude, offensive comments.

But on the north side of Müller Strasse, which was several kilometers long, one felt as though one were out of the city. Here new neighborhoods rose, modest but well-kept Bauhaus-style buildings, and on the side streets, there were little wooden sheds with tiny gardens. Their happy owners grew flowers and vegetables for their households.

Our house stood on the border between the old, derelict quarter and the new neighborhood, and the shop was in the same building. Papa sold leather for shoe repairs and all the tools and instruments a shoemaker needed, as well as shoe polish and shoelaces. In short, it was a kind of "shoemakers' department store." From the store, there were several stairs leading down to the basement in which there was leather of every kind and quality, and in the back of the store, behind the door, was a little niche with a sink and faucet. On a little spirit burner, Papa would make tea.

He would drink endless cups of tea every day while sucking a sugar cube.

For work, Papa wore a yellow robe, and in his pocket, he had a special round knife to cut the skins. The shoemakers would buy on credit and were late settling their debts because most of their customers were unemployed and had difficulty paying them. "Meister" was what they would call Papa, a title credited to someone who successfully finished his apprenticeship and was allowed to teach new students. And indeed, Papa would teach many unemployed who couldn't afford to pay for shoe repairs. He would advise them on the best leather to choose to repair the soles of their shoes and how to get the job done themselves. I was a witness when he told one of them, "You chose low-quality leather. Don't buy this merchandise."

Usually, the buyers weren't in a hurry, and when they came to buy leather, they'd linger to discuss their daily problems as well as matters of the world. Sometimes, the shop became a place where anarchists, Trotskyists, and communists argued. I spent a lot of time there and helped my father hold the bales of leather—which he cut into squares—absorbed their smell, and knew my way around the merchandise. Mostly, I listened to the customers' conversations.

***

Fifty years later, when I visited Berlin, I found Papa's shop, which had become a jewelry shop. The door to the building was the same one I remembered: brown, heavy, and impressive. The house had a layer of new paint, and on the balconies, geraniums bloomed. I didn't enter the building itself. Several more years passed, and in February 2003, I visited Berlin again with my oldest son and his wife. Once again, I returned to the building that was once my home. We climbed up the stairs and hesitantly knocked on the door. After several minutes, when we didn't hear a thing, we turned to go. Just then, a young man arrived and offered to open the door and show us the apartment, which was now empty and for rent.

I was brimming with excitement when I entered the apartment that I left as a child, sixty-four years ago. It felt as though time had frozen. Nothing had changed in the apartment. The high ceiling was ornamented with cast flowers, the unique fireplace covered with china tiles, and even the little window seat where I would sit, my nose buried in a book, taking advantage of the last light before the *Shabbat* came in, was still there. I went to the park named after the poet Schiller, and just around the corner, I found the same cart that sold fruit, in the exact same place. Here, Mother would buy bananas and oranges for the road. In the park, I discovered the same hidden, romantic niches and arbors covered with white and pink wild roses. Just the same as many years ago.

I visited the big park called *Rehbergen* ("Deer Hills") again, and on the way there, I came across small wooden shacks with dahlias blooming in front of them. Brown squirrels cavorted in the park and cracked acorns, while timid deer skipped in the grass. Only the trees had grown in the meantime, and their shade now was wider and deeper. Not much had changed about the lake where we used to swim in the summer and where I made my first ice skating attempt in the winter. What was new was the boat marina.

An entire world had been destroyed. Faith in man, culture,

and progress had been undermined. A third of our people went up in smoke, and those who survived carried deep scars that left their mark on the second generation as well. And here in Berlin, nothing had changed.

***

The Nazis came to power in January 1933 through democratic elections. The German chancellor, old Marshal Hindenburg, invited Hitler to establish a new government. Three weeks later, in February, the German Reichstag went up in flames. The fire, which some assume the Nazis were behind, was an excuse to dissolve the Reichstag, to ban all parties, and to enact emergency laws that restricted freedom of speech. By April, shops owned by Jews were boycotted. On the sidewalk, before Papa's store, someone wrote in huge letters, "Germans don't buy from the Jewish pig!"

The unemployed were recruited for jobs outside of the city and disappeared from the streets. They proudly wore the brown uniform, with the shiny boots and the swastika on their sleeve, and marched in formation. On Sundays, at dawn, swarms of brown-uniformed people marched down our streets and sang marching songs. "Today Germany, tomorrow the whole world!"

There was something hypnotic about it, both threatening and mesmerizing. It was frightening to see so many people wearing brown uniforms, walking in sync, in straight rows, waving flags, and pounding on drums. At school, in the morning before entering the classroom, all the children gathered in the yard, and the swastika flag was raised to the top of the pole. The principal would shout while raising his hand, "Heil Hitler!" and the girls would repeat loudly after him, "Heil Hitler!" Only I, an eight-year-old child, stood there, still and quiet, waiting for the assembly to end.

In German lessons, new subjects were added to composition writing, such as "With Hitler—toward a strong Germany" or "We all listen to Hitler's speech." I wrote such a composition as well, based on a speech that appeared in the newspaper. My teacher was impressed, read it before the entire class, and also showed it to the principal. Perhaps she forgot that a little Jewish girl wrote the best composition. The matter died quietly.

Frequently, when I left the school, boys would bully me, hit me, and sing derogatory songs about Jews. I hoped one of the passersby would interfere, scold the bullies, and rush to help me. But nothing happened. German citizens didn't see, didn't hear, and didn't know what was happening around them. I would run home, to Papa's shop, and he would say, "It will all pass. The German people won't put up for long with this madman's rule."

Papa was wrong. Perhaps his optimism was aided by the fact that the shoemakers remained loyal to him and continued buying from him, some of them out of fondness, and some of them because they didn't have a choice. There wasn't another store like his in the area. Our financial situation wasn't great, but it remained steady.

In the summer, as in previous years, we went away for several weeks to the Baltic Sea. Mother took her cooking utensils with her, to keep kosher, and we rented a room in one of the fishing villages. Papa would come to visit us only on the weekends. We spent time on the beach from morning till evening, splashing in the water, playing in the sand. Sometimes I helped pick fruit; in the yard of one of the farmers, there were plum trees, apple trees, and tiny berries that grew on bushes. Sometimes I'd go out to the fields with him and return on a wagon piled with fragrant harvest. In the evening, Mother would buy smoked fish with an alluring smell and fresh bread baked by the farmers. Weeks of simple joy meandered by, causing us to forget the fears that darkened the skies in Berlin.

The three sisters, Ruth, Betty and Bronia, on a sled in in 1937.

THE OTHER WORLD IN THE EAST

Every year, Papa would travel to Poland to visit his father's grave and call on his mother and brothers. I was nine the first time I traveled with him to meet my grandmother and the rest of my family there. I remember taking in the sights beyond the border, the different landscape. It was October and the days were cold and rainy, but the farmers in the fields worked barefoot while the women wrapped their feet with rags. A strange man passed by us, his face covered with a filthy scarf tied on the top of his head. My father explained to me that the man was suffering from a toothache. I saw people wearing rags, with poles on their shoulders, carrying buckets of water. Sights of poverty here were different than the poverty I knew from Berlin. There, poverty was institutionalized, with welfare services and unemployment compensation.

At the train station in Krakow, my father left me for a moment, and two yeshiva students with beards and sideburns approached me and said that Papa asked them to fetch our suitcases. Luckily, he came back right on time and they ran away. I wondered how religious people could be thieves. These were the first cracks in my innocence.

Outside the station, dozens of coachmen pulled on my father's coat in a wild competition to decide who would take us. A loud argument developed regarding the price. A strange and unfamiliar world.

Krakow was a glittery city with elegant women, elegant just like the apartment where my father's half-sisters lived. He was not very close to them, so we just stopped there for some refreshments and continued to the city of Jaslo, where my aunt Tova, my mother's older sister, lived. Her two-room apartment faced the market. Aunt Tova was a tall, slender, pretty woman. Her face was long, her forehead high. Her husband was much shorter than her and round. He was a pleasant man. They had seven children. They made a very modest living, and my aunt helped the family's livelihood by making wigs. I remember the atmosphere there as relaxed and close. The youngest son was summoned to demonstrate his proficiency in the Gemara and received praise.

We said goodbye to the Schild family, and that was the first and last time I saw them. Their fate was similar to the fate of the rest of my relatives in Poland: annihilation. Only two of their sons, Meir and Israel, who immigrated to Palestine in the thirties, were saved.

We continued to Tarnów, to visit Uncle Pinhas, my mother's brother. He and his wife lived in a one-room apartment that contained only a bed, a closet, and a bare table. The room was gloomy, without even one picture, a colorful curtain, or an ornamental object. She lay in their bed, covered from head to toe. They were childless. Their house was cold, the atmosphere chilling. Pinhas's greatest wish was to accumulate the means to write a Torah scroll that he would leave, instead of children, after he was gone. He was an impressive man: tall, very thin, with a black beard and dark, smoldering eyes. Later, I saw a painting by El Greco and remembered my uncle's tortured face.

My paternal grandmother had a little wooden house surrounded by a small plot of land on the outskirts of the city of Nowy Sacz. Grandmother Perla lived there with Aunt Hinda and her four-year-old daughter. Grandmother was a tiny woman, thin with a delicate, pale face. Hinda, on the other hand, who had divorced her husband, was stout with a stern face. Every morning, she'd head to work, leaving her daughter under Grandmother's supervision. We stayed there for more than a week, during which Papa left to visit his brother Yehuda, who lived with his wife and four children in a little village called Bobowa. I refused to accompany him on this visit. Thus, I never had the pleasure of meeting Yehuda, my father's favorite brother.

I never told Papa why I refused to go with him. In Poland, until we arrived at Grandmother Perla's house, I became traumatized by the bathrooms, which usually gave off a horrific stench. It was different at Grandmother's house. They had an outhouse, a little wooden shed with a floor covered with white lime and a wooden seat over a hole. It was scrubbed clean and smelled of soap. On a nail on the wall there were precisely cut newspapers. This was a treasure I refused to leave.

This is how my family's story in Poland ends. No one knows how, when, and where everyone was murdered.

***

From the day she was born, my sister Betty suffered from a persistent intestinal disease. Constant diarrhea caused her to be underweight and to contract infectious diseases. This was before the age of antibiotics, and every illness went on for many days. Mother was extremely worried about Betty, while I, blessed with robust health and an appetite, got much less attention from her.

As was customary in many well-to-do families, we were connected to a doctor who did regular house calls, who guided Mother in matters of food, clothing, and hygiene. Papa, by the way, had his own firm opinions about a healthy lifestyle. Therefore, we lived our lives according to modern research and old-time traditional customs. For example, it was believed that fried food wasn't good for your health; therefore, our entire menu was based on cooked food. Bread was edible for only one day after it was baked. The bedroom was never heated, not even in the winter, when the temperatures were below zero. Water could not be drunk after eating fruit. Ice cream, which I loved, was served only on the hottest days, which meant only several days in the summer. Papa believed in walks when it was freezing cold and in any weather, while Mother believed in sun baths. They both believed in the damage caused by drafts. Every evening, we received a tablespoon of fresh lemon juice to provide vitamin C and a teaspoon of honey for strength and immunization. Why? Just because. Mother also claimed that spinach had almost magical properties and was crucial for our development. Betty would cry and spit out the spinach. The table, the chair, and everything around was covered in green, but Mother wouldn't give in.

Treating a fever had its own regular pattern. First, we had to sweat. The method involved lying in bed, covered with blankets, and drinking hot tea until our entire bodies were drenched with sweat, a process that sometimes went on for a long while and was torturous. Then, pajamas and sheets were quickly changed. On sick days, there was a regular procedure: morning, noon, and evening with lemon and toast and strict bedrest. After such treatment, I'd get better quickly, but not my sister. I especially remember one night; Betty burned with fever and had difficulty breathing. She couldn't swallow a drop of water. The doctor looked helpless, as she feared diphtheria was hovering in the air—a children's disease that killed many young children at the time. My parents called a prominent pediatrician, and the entire night, the light burned in our apartment. Mother tried to ease Betty's suffering by adhering to the advice the two doctors had given her, while Papa paced the room and read from Psalms. At dawn, the fever finally broke and Betty started breathing more easily, thanks to the doctors and Mother's devotion. And perhaps because of Papa's prayers?

In the winter of 1934, the house doctor visited us frequently and held whispered conferences with Mother in the bedroom. I remember them saying that Mother was in "a special condition" and that it was a bad time for that to happen. January 1935 was very cold. The temperature was 15 Celsius below zero, which was a rare occurrence in Berlin. Our windows were covered with frost, and the large tiled stove that burned coal didn't heat the apartment adequately. Early one morning, Papa woke us up and told us Mother went away to bring us a special present and until she returned, we'd stay with Uncle Marcus and Aunt Mali.

Uncle Marcus (Mordechai), Mother's brother, was very tall, like all the men of the Neuwirth family. He walked slightly hunched, as though ashamed of his height. His face was long and chiseled and his forehead high, and he constantly thought of work and business. His wife, Aunt Mali, was a tiny, plump blonde, full of good will and small talk. Their apartment was a hive of constant activity, with guests who ate, drank, and wandered about the many rooms while negotiating with Uncle Marcus. Amid this commotion, their four children ran around noisily, fighting and making up.

Our aunt welcomed us with open arms. My sister and I were freezing from the journey, but it wasn't long before we warmed up thanks to their central heating. Aunt Mali poured me a cup of coffee and added heaped teaspoons of sugar. I refused because I was taught at home to drink it without sugar, but Mali wouldn't take no for an answer. "Sweet is good. Drink, children, drink." And she placed a generous slice of cake on my plate, one that I didn't like. Before I managed to eat half, another slice was piled on my plate. Until her last day, my aunt was known for her poor cooking skills, and I'll never forget the most disgusting dish she'd invented: beef goulash covered with spinach. I tried to swallow that atrocity out of politeness and was attacked by nausea like I'd never known before. Betty burst into bitter tears and was exempt from the punishment.

My uncle's house was full of appliances: a telephone, a piano, a typewriter, even an electric coffee grinder. In the evening, my aunt and uncle would go out to do whatever it was they did. The children would all pretend to be asleep, but the minute the door closed behind them, everyone jumped out of bed. First of all, we'd try to break the pantry's lock. We knew that all the good stuff saved for the guests was in there. Then we banged on the piano, typed on the typewriter, and to make a long story short, we had a ball. When the guard on duty gave us a sign, everyone scampered back to bed and pretended to be in a deep, sweet sleep.

In the morning, waking everyone up to go to school was hard work. My aunt would shout and pull off their blankets, but it was in vain. She even poured cold water on the face of her eldest son, Sigmund (Sisha), my cousin who was one year older than me. They couldn't instill discipline in Sisha, and a year later, they sent him to study in a yeshiva in Frankfurt. Although no one managed to discipline him, Zisha and his three sons became orthodox Jews.

Papa came to visit us and told us that Mother brought us a gift, a baby, and her name was Bronia.

I'd never before heard the name Bronia and loved the sound of it. The entire family congratulated Papa, although they were slightly mocking. Maybe because they knew it wasn't easy to prepare dowries for three girls. Papa was proud, although slightly disappointed that he didn't get his much-longed-for son this time. When we returned home, we found Mother in bed with a sweet baby next to her. As was customary at the time, Mother was on bedrest for an entire month. I loved that mischievous, lively baby from the first minute, with her little hands with tiny pink fingers, her fluff of hair, and the fragrant milky smell of her body. I was ten years old, and I wondered if I'd ever love my own children this way.

***

In 1933, the Jewish community in Berlin had more than one hundred and sixty thousand members, out of a population of 3.5 million. In other parts of Germany, there were communities that were much older, but there was no doubt that Berlin was the center of attraction for Jews from all over Germany as well as Jews who arrived from the "East," from Poland and Russia, and were called "*Ostjuden*." Many Jewish artists, whose names and fame had spread beyond Germany's borders, made important contributions in the fields of theater, art, music, and literature, as well as science, medicine, and philosophy. Large publishing houses in Germany, and a majority of the newspapers, were in Jewish hands. Berlin's large department stores belonged to Jews, among them the prestigious department store Israel.

This rich and established community provided not only religious answers; in addition to lavish synagogues scattered all over the city, there were also schools, two very good hospitals, and establishments for social welfare, such as retirement homes, orphanages, and social services for those in need. During the years 1933–1938, the activities of all the Jewish establishments expanded and eased the hardships of the Jewish public. The Jewish community's high school, in which four hundred and fifty students studied before Hitler's rise to power, received double the number of students during those years.

In 1935, I finished four years of primary school and continued my education in the Jewish high school on Grosse Hamburger Strasse. It was an institution recognized by the authorities, and the tuition was much lower than what the private schools charged. I felt good there. After the pressure and loneliness of primary school, I felt as free as a bird. No more morning assembly with students shouting "Heil Hitler," no more Nazi songs about knives spilling Jewish blood. I felt good, although I had to get up early to catch the tram, which passed by our house at 7:10 a.m.

The classes were crowded, with up to fifty girls in each classroom, the curriculum was busy, and school went on until the afternoon hours. I accepted everything with love. Most of the girls lived in the area and would go home at noon, while I'd stay in the classroom with stale sandwiches. But as far as I was concerned, this difficulty was nothing compared to the nice feeling of unity and the interest I found in school.

The school was located in Berlin's ancient quarter and stood on the first lot purchased by the community, three hundred years before. The entrance was a lovely little garden, and in it, on a high pedestal, was the bust of the head of Moses Mendelssohn, a philosopher and the pioneer of the idea of Jewish emancipation who claimed, "Be a Jew in your home, and a human being when you leave." On the wall of the foyer, there was a motto written in bright large gold letters, "May the school be a workshop of humanity." And those who climbed halfway up the staircase came across a huge photo of the statue *Moses* by Michelangelo. The entire place exuded culture.

On the building's upper floor was a large and lavish auditorium in which the students would assemble at the beginning and end of the school year and on festive occasions. On the walls were portraits of generations of dignitaries of the Jewish community, staring thoughtfully out of the heavy gilded frames. Concerts were held in this hall, played by students of the school. I wasn't used to listening to classical music, and during these events, I was bored senseless and more than once found myself braiding the hair of girls sitting in front of me.

Girls and boys studied separately and spent ten o'clock recess together. The older students would go for a walk in the park that bordered the school. In the park was the first Jewish cemetery of Berlin as well as the grave of Moses Mendelssohn. The students would stroll among the rickety headstones covered with ivy and moss and wander along the hidden paths among the tangled bushes. During exercise lessons, the students practiced running there in order to receive a medal. In short, the old cemetery was full of life.

School was conducted according to the mandatory curriculum for all high schools, with the addition of Jewish literature and history. We read the books of the German authors Schiller and Goethe as well as Shalom Aleichem and Peretz. In history, we learned about the legendary king Barbarossa, about Frederick the Great, king of Prussia, and also about ibn Gabirol, about the Golden Age in Spain, and about the Inquisition. We learned about medieval troubadours and the poems of Yehuda Halevy. We learned English intensively as well as modern Hebrew, as opposed to Hebrew with an Ashkenazi dialect, which was used only for praying. French was an optional subject. And I managed to reach a level of fluent reading and knowledge of grammar. I could read Hebrew and understand the stories of the righteous Joseph in the stories of Genesis.

I attended school for a few years only, until the age of thirteen and a half, but those years were full of interest. At the time, I would lose myself in reading. Gusti, my cousin, who was three years older than me, helped me choose books, and I still remember some of them: *Ivanhoe*, *The Last Days of Pompeii*, *Ben-Hur*, *Crime and Punishment*, *The Revival*, *Anna Karenina*, books by Stefan Zweig and Knut Hamsun, and *All Quiet on the Western Front* by Remarque.

Famous Jewish stage actors, who lost their source of livelihood because of the Nazi racial laws, founded a theater for adolescents, and like the rest of my classmates, I bought an annual subscription to these plays. They put on plays by Shakespeare, Molière, Goldoni, and Kleist, as well as a play about Shabbetai Tzvi. Jews were forbidden from entering cinemas and theaters as well as swimming pools and ice rinks. At the entrance to the cafés, signs were hung reading, "Jews and dogs aren't wanted here." So instead, the Jewish community organized its own cultural activities.

During World War I, the Jews of Germany fought in the German Army. Twelve thousand Jews lost their lives. There was a memorial wall in every synagogue with the names of the fallen community members. Among our teachers were many who served in the army during that war and saw themselves as Germans of Jewish faith. They worked hard to convey that perception of their identity to their students.

On the other hand, many of the students came from families that emigrated from Eastern Europe and had roots deeply embedded in Judaism. They, myself among them, knew we were born in Germany, that German was our language, and an important part of our culture was German. Nevertheless, we weren't Germans, but Jews. I remember a song I learned in Hebrew lessons. Its words expressed what I believed in and wanted to achieve.

> "Oh, until when will our people live,
> Without a country, wandering here and there?
> Until its sons will unite as a people,
> Until they will learn the language,
> And return to their country."

***

Fifty years later, I returned to visit my old school in Berlin. Dadi, my husband, who studied at the same institute during the years 1927–1935, accompanied me. We went to Berlin, which was separated by the still-standing wall. The school was in East Berlin, and to get there, we had to go through a tedious procedure. Among other things, we had to procure a permit to stay in East Berlin for one day only, until midnight. It was a summer day, but the sun wasn't strong enough to overcome the gray gloominess and the neglect that prevailed everywhere. There were few passersby on the street, and a couple of Trabant cars drove down the once bustling wide avenues. The only colorful decorations were huge posters of the party leaders on the walls of houses. Our feet led us of their own volition to Grösse Hamburger Strasse, a street whose corner once housed a toy shop with nineteen display windows that had set my imagination on fire and made me late for school more than once. Now, all I saw was a derelict, sad structure, its windows boarded up.

We stood before the school gate, next to the little garden that was now covered with weeds, and looked at the remains of the gray stone on which Mendelssohn's bust once stood. Over the gate, covered with whitewash, one could still read, "High School of the Jewish Community." Dadi was searching for the right angle to take a picture of the gate with the inscription when an old man stopped next to us and asked us what we were taking a picture of.

"We both went to school here before the war," I said. "Yes, yes. I remember. Those were difficult days." Really? Difficult for whom?

The man was curious to hear where we came from. We told him.

"Israel? Ah, *Palestina*! That's very far." "Only a four-hour flight," I said.

After several minutes, the man took a big watch out of his

pocket and mumbled, "I must go home. My old lady is waiting with potatoes for lunch."

We entered the building, which had become a vocational school. The walls were bare, the plaster peeling. There wasn't even one picture, not even a plant. Everything was gray. The stairwell with the lovely wooden bannister and brass buttons survived, but its shine had dimmed. There was the principal's office, the same room. On a window with a cracked pane someone had glued a sign that read, "Administration Wing." We climbed another story and searched for the assembly hall. In the big hall, folding chairs were scattered haphazardly. Here as well, the walls were bare. Nothing remained from its former splendor and glory.

We went down to the yard where we played at recess and walked to the nearby cemetery. In the yard was a pile of black coal, and it seemed as though the air we were breathing was blacker than black. The cemetery was covered with garbage and junk, and broken headstones leaned on the wall. A sign in German and Hebrew indicated that there used to be a Jewish cemetery there. What had happened to my classmates? I knew about only two who left Germany in time. In the retirement home next to our school, the Gestapo had set up their headquarters, and here, during the years 1943–1945, the last Jews of Berlin were gathered and sent to the death camps.

***

Back to my childhood, to 1933. In the building where our apartment was, over Papa's shop, lived all sorts of important people—doctors, other professionals, and businesspeople. After Hitler's rise to power, they and their families stopped greeting us when we met in the stairwell. My little sister Bronia would greet them every time with a cheerful good morning accompanied by a graceful curtsy, but they didn't even blink back. Only the common police officer, who lived on the fourth floor beneath the roof, felt the need to apologize. As he checked nervously to see if anyone saw him, he addressed my mother. "I have nothing against you. On the contrary, I actually like you and your family. But please understand, Frau Schütz, I have a wife and children. I cannot risk my livelihood." Mother understood.

Papa's regular clients grew fewer. Jews were officially obligated to write the name of the shop owner in big white letters on any Jewish store. On the window of our shop, Papa's name was written—Josef Schütz—which had a clear, German sound. Papa's name confused the uniformed Nazis. They would enter our store and yell, "Heil Hitler!" and Papa would answer with quiet restraint, "Good morning, gentlemen."

Things at home became more and more grim, and for hours and days my parents discussed the issue of if, when, and where they should buy me a winter coat. In the past, we had only fixed the soles of our shoes. Now, I had a patch on my upper part as well. Sometimes, the only thing we ate for lunch was porridge with sugar and cinnamon, and at dinner, Mother would spread butter on a slice of bread, with one movement smearing and another removing the surplus butter. On the bread, she'd put a slice of tomato with onion.

In the winter, we partially heated only one room. Rent

payments for the apartment and the store weighed on us heavily, and the monthly stipend Papa sent to his sister and three children was burdensome. I received a discount for a third of my tuition fees, and my parents had a hard time paying the remaining two thirds. At the beginning of the school year, I tried to sell my old textbooks. I wanted to use the money to buy books for the new school year, but I wasn't very good at business negotiations, and from year to year, my books became more and more tattered.

Mother became very burdened with the household chores, and it was obvious to me that I had to help. I was in charge of grocery shopping and shopping at the greengrocer. Since we didn't have a refrigerator, we bought milk every day, and I remember the milkman skillfully pouring the milk into the jug I'd brought. With German precision he poured the milk, not a drop more, but not a drop less. He was a kind man that milkman, and sometimes he'd give me a sweet. At home, I'd put the milk on the fire, and I had to keep an eye on it so that, God forbid, it wouldn't boil over. Otherwise, the revolting smell of burned milk would spread all over the apartment.

It was a different story with the vegetables. Mother was never happy with the fruit and vegetables I brought, and sometimes she demanded I return to the greengrocer and change the merchandise. When I refused, she'd start shouting and sometimes even raised her hand at me. She became very tense, and it was hard to please her. After school and during the holidays, I took care of my little sisters. We took walks in the park, and I played with them at home. In any event, I didn't have Jewish friends my age in the neighborhood.

I taught Betty to write and read before she started first grade and went over exercises that I myself had trouble performing. For my father, I ran errands to the post office or visited shoemakers who owed him money and promised to pay.

Then, suddenly, Papa fell ill and was hospitalized; I don't know why. Perhaps he couldn't stand the pressure of those difficult times. When Mother went to visit him in the hospital, I manned the shop. There were clients who asked, "How old are you, child?" and I unhesitatingly replied, "Fifteen," even though I wasn't yet thirteen.

On Sundays, when the shop was closed and there was no school, we went to visit Papa in the hospital. That vigorous man lay in bed, pale, defeated, and sad. In the evening, before I went to sleep, I prayed to God that he'd protect my father and give him strength so he'd be able to come home and be the father I knew. And yet, the general atmosphere of the hospital enchanted me greatly. The quiet, the halls soaked with the smell of carbolic, the signs with names of the departments in incomprehensible Latin, the doctors and their important expressions, and the nurses with their starched, white uniforms. All this seemed to me very mysterious and interesting. I thought I might like to be a nurse when I grew up, yet nevertheless, I wondered whether I'd be able to laugh and be happy if I'd be in close proximity to daily suffering and pain.

In the city square, huge posters appeared, portraying Jews in a monstrous-demonic manner accompanied by slogans such as "Jews are our disaster" or "Jews, like rats, live on the blood and sweat of the German people." These pictures made me nauseous with terror. I was gripped with a fear that maybe we really were subhuman. On street corners, the newspaper *Der Stürmer* was distributed. The newspaper was full of propaganda regarding "the contamination of the race," including pornographic descriptions that cautioned against sexual abuse of the German women by Jewish vermin.

Every so often, new decrees were imposed that deprived Jews of their civil rights. Jews of desired professions, who owned property or had ties abroad, managed to leave Germany back in 1933. But as the time went by, the European countries closed their borders. Visas to the United States were almost impossible to obtain. The British Mandate government distributed very few permits to immigrate to Palestine. In 1938, the situation was desperate. Papa tried to obtain an entry visa to Palestine and was rejected. He was willing to immigrate even to Hong Kong, but it didn't work out.

The Jewish newspapers advertised vocational programs that would help one to change professions. Philosophy professors studied carpentry, high-society women studied hairdressing and manicure. I was especially impressed by a course to create chocolate delicacies and hoped my mother would attend the program. There was a new section in the newspaper: Jewish families in the United States offering to foster Jewish children. One ad especially set fire to my imagination. A family from Texas with a big house, a garden, and a swimming pool, horses, and dogs, wanted to adopt a girl my age. I showed my parents the ad and asked if we should contact them. Mother started crying, and Papa was terribly angry and said, "Our family will stay together, no matter what." I was ashamed and said no more.

Our close family became smaller and smaller from year to year, and we were extremely lonely. My parents had an odd approach to death; they didn't dare say the explicit word and barely mentioned the deceased. Grandfather passed away in 1932 from lung cancer, and while he lay dying, no one told me he was sick or took me to visit him in the hospital. One day, when I came home from school, the mirror in the hall was covered with a cloth, and Mother sat barefoot on a low stool sobbing. Papa tried to soothe her and said, "Berta! You mustn't cry like that. This is God's will. *Baruch dayan emet*!" (Blessed is the true judge.)

Nobody paid me any attention. What did a seven-year-old child understand?

My uncle Max moved to a training farm in Czechoslovakia, and in 1934, he immigrated to Palestine. His twin sister, Betty, married young and moved to Stettin with her husband, Paul, and after a year, Max managed to bring them to Israel. My cousin Batya and her brother Jacob also immigrated, as part of the "Youth *Aliyah*" organization. They took the train from Berlin to Trieste, a port city in Italy, and from there boarded a ship to Haifa. I can still see the scene of our farewell. It was at the train station in Berlin. My aunt Chatchah cried, and Papa told her, "You should be happy they're leaving. We, the ones who are staying, are those to be cried over." How right he was.

My aunt and her daughter Gusti hid in Berlin during the war. In 1943, they were caught and sent to the Ravensbrück concentration camp. The Red Army liberated them at the end of the war.

The weekdays of 1938 were gray and gloomy. Perhaps that's why the holidays seemed prettier and more festive than usual. My favorite holiday was Passover, and preparations started right after Purim. Mother filled a bulbous clay pot with slices of beetroot and water. Four weeks later, the beetroot started fermenting and a layer of mold covered the liquid. We girls and even Papa couldn't stand this potion, and it seemed as though even Mother didn't like it. But on Passover, Uncle Marcus came to visit, and the minute he came, he asked, "*Nu*, Berta, is there any borscht?" and drank one cup after another. It was for him that Mother prepared this year after year.

Cooking pots kept especially for Passover were brought down from the attic. In the pantry, an abundance of kosher food was piled, and not a corner of the house escaped a thorough cleaning. Mother would take all the clothes out of the closet and turn out every pocket of every garment in case a crumb of leavened food hid there. One day before the holiday, the stove was heated until it turned red, and all the dishes and silverware were immersed in boiling water. When night fell, it was time to remove the leavened bread. Papa would hold the candle, while Mother, holding a feather and a dustpan, collected all the breadcrumbs she made sure to scatter beforehand in different places. This was the only time I saw Papa help with the household chores.

The next day we would eat a quick breakfast. By ten, all the leavened food would be thrown out of the house, but eating the *matzah* was allowed only in the evening, during the *seder*.

The house would fill with the wonderful smell of dishes Mother made for the holiday feast. My sisters and I circled her hungrily, hoping to taste some of the things she cooked.

In the evening, the table was set with silverware and thin, fragile china plates, dishes saved especially for the holiday. A Passover dish painted blue was set in the middle of the table, and in it, *haroset* (a mixture of fruits, wine or honey, and nuts), *maror* (bitter herbs), and charred bone (symbolizes the lamb that Jews sacrificed as the special Passover offering), and three *matzahs*, each *matzah* in its own place, covered with a gold-embroidered napkin. A bottle of Carmel wine made in Palestine stood by a decorated silver goblet. For us girls, Mother prepared sweet golden raisin wine, which was a delicacy. In a five-armed candlestick, white candles burned.

Papa sat in the recliner, leaning on pillows, wearing a silver-embroidered white cape and on his head a white-embroidered yarmulke. Mother brought him a bowl and a jug of water to wash his hands. He said a blessing and started reading the *Haggadah*. Once in a while, I glanced at Elijah the Prophet's glass, and I could've sworn that it was emptying. As the ceremony proceeded, we stood and Papa opened the front door. From the dark stairwell, a cold blast of wind entered the apartment. "Pour out thy wrath upon the nations!" we whispered with intent. I trembled, and perhaps I wasn't the only one. After the soup and the fish, I was filled with a sweet weariness, and the singing mixed with my dreams. When the time came to steal the *Afikoman*, I was already sound asleep.

In *Shavuot* of 1938, like every year, the house was decorated with green branches, bright-blue star-thistle flowers, and stalks of grain, and Mother would prepare dairy dishes. I loved the taste of the cheese-filled dumplings in butter sauce. In the synagogue, they read the story of Ruth, one I loved.

Summer vacation that year was sad. Jews weren't allowed to do anything. Fortunately, somehow the prohibitions didn't include the huge lawn in the park next to our house. The park was open to the public only during vacations, and during the rest of the year, it was explicitly forbidden to go there.

This time, for some strange reason, they forgot to put up the sign that read "Jews and dogs aren't wanted here," and every morning we'd go out to play ball there. Mother accompanied us, carrying a basket bursting with sandwiches and fruit. She had a weakness for fruit. Our pantry was always full of sour yellow cherries, sweet black cherries, blueberries that painted our tongues blue and that we ate in sweetened milk, juicy pears, plums of every kind, and various types of strawberries. Perhaps she wanted to compensate for the lack of meat in our diet because of the prohibition of kosher slaughtering in Germany.

When summer vacation ended, I was happy to go back to school and see my friends. But then I found out that many girls had left. Some of the teachers also managed to leave Germany, and the school hadn't found their replacements.

The New Year arrived. Papa said the blessing, gave us an apple in honey, and wished us a good, sweet year. But our hearts were heavy. We knew we shouldn't expect a good year, but we had no idea it would be the last holiday we would spend together and that soon, each of us would go his or her own way and to his or her own fate.

Things got worse. In October 1938, Germany invaded Austria. The Austrians and Germans went on a rampage against the Jews of Vienna. Before that, Germany conquered the Sudetenland in Czechoslovakia. The Germans were drunk with victory and full of enthusiasm for Hitler's reign. There were rumors that men of Polish citizenship would be imprisoned, so Papa slept for a week at the home of one of his German colleagues, who was a shoemaker and a sworn communist. He returned home on a Thursday night because he missed us and wanted to spend that *Shabbat* at home. At four in the morning, we heard pounding on the front door and loud shouting. I cringed in bed in fear, and Mother asked, "Who's there?"

"Gestapo! Open up."

My two little sisters burst into tears. Two Gestapo men with black uniforms stood in our hallway and told Papa to get up and get dressed. I also got dressed and ran down the stairs. A black car stood before the building. Papa was shoved into the car, and I clung to the door and gripped it while screaming, "Papa, Papa!"

The uniformed man shoved me, and I fell on the sidewalk. At that moment, I knew I would never see my father again. I felt a bitter hatred and a desire for revenge. It was the first and last time I wanted to choke and kill every German I saw.

***

On the *Shabbat* eve, Papa's chair remained empty. Mother blessed the *challah* bread, and we sobbed bitterly. Papa's incarceration was part of an operation: At the end of October 1938, seventeen thousand Jews of Polish citizenship were exiled from Germany. The exiled Jews were allowed to take only a small bundle of personal belongings and some money. They were taken to the Polish border. The Polish government refused to let them into their territory, and in the dead of night, the Germans used violence, threats, and shooting in the air to force the prisoners to cross the border.

Most of those Jews arrived at Zbaszyn, a small border town. Thousands of Jews crowded there, in that small territory, without food or water or sanitary conditions. They sat there, exposed to the elements, without a roof over their head. Winter approached and added to their torment. The Polish government wouldn't allow them to leave the town, in an attempt to force the Germans to take them back to Germany. After some time, Jewish institutes organized aid for them.

Papa stayed at Zbaszyn all winter, and at the beginning of summer, he managed to make his way to Krakow. In one of the few letters we received from him, he begged Mother to find a way to send him some money to survive. When the war broke out on September 1, 1939, we lost touch with Papa, entirely and forever.

***

I'll skip several years forward. The first time I saw my mother after the war was in 1950, when she came to visit the kibbutz.

In 1955, I visited Mother in London for the first time, and only then, she told me that, during all those years, she lived in hope that Papa would return. She also showed me a roll of a high-quality English textile that she'd bought to have a suit made for him. She told me she met a man who knew Papa in Buchenwald, and he told her, "I wish Josef Schütz had survived instead of me. He would have found his wife and daughters, while I lost my entire family and the desire to live." That's what the man said and added no more.

Recently, I came across an official document that stated that in September 1944, Papa had been transferred to Buchenwald Camp in Germany, and in January 1945, to Bergen-Belsen. There, according to the German document, "he disappeared without a trace." This information shocked me greatly; in 1945, I was already in Israel, in a safe place, and I never even imagined my father was alive. Was it his faith in God that sustained him? Or perhaps his hope that he'd find his family? He probably survived all those years in the camps thanks to his profession as a shoemaker, for the Germans needed professionals.

Several more years passed, and I was a mother of adult sons and a grandmother. My sister Betty and her husband donated money to build a room in an educational institution for boys in Jerusalem, in memory of Papa. Many people attended the inaugural reception, both from Israel and abroad. We received a comprehensive explanation regarding the institute's educational activity. There were speeches and thanks. My sister received an intricate box with a key to the room she had donated, and we went to remove the veil from the brass plate on which our father's name was engraved. Right then, I felt my entire body tremble and I burst into tears. We stood there, Betty and I, and wept like two abandoned girls. It was the first time in my life I cried and mourned the loss of my father.

***

One week after the Jews with Polish citizenship were driven out of Germany, Herschel Feibel Grynszpan, a young Jewish man, assassinated the Nazi German diplomat in Paris. This resulted in *Kristallnacht*, the anti-Semitic pogrom that took place on November 10, 1938. All over Germany, synagogues were torched, display windows of Jewish shops were shattered and looted. The incited mob threw furniture from Jewish apartments through the windows, and thousands of Jews were beaten, sent to concentration camps, or murdered. Until then, the Jewish public had been humiliated and stripped bare of its civil rights, but now, the added message was that Jewish blood was cheap. As for us, we were the only Jewish family in the area, our family name sounded German, and thus, we were almost forgotten during the *Kristallnacht*. It was only toward morning that someone remembered us and one stone shattered our window and landed inside, on the rug.

Several days after that night of horror, I went to school to meet my teachers and classmates. The tramcar passed by the big synagogue on Oranienburger Strasse, the most magnificent synagogue in Berlin, with a golden dome in its center and the Star of David that was seen from a distance.

A year before, I'd visited the synagogue and was impressed by the splendor, the colorful windows, the sounds of the organ that filled the hall, and the choir of boys that sang as the cantor conducted them. Some of the visitors came in cars and parked them in front of the building. The synagogue visitors wore tiny prayer shawls, and the rabbi wore a long mantle and a black hat. All this was very different from the small family synagogue I was used to. Although Papa was an orthodox Jew, he wanted me to know other religious movements in Judaism. Therefore, he chose to visit this synagogue, but on Hanukkah and not during an important holiday. I remember that the rabbi, Dr. Joachim Prinz, finished his Mishna with a Hebrew sentence that, for some reason, was engraved in my memory: "*Baruch meshaneh eitim.*" (Blessed be the one who changes the times.)

In November 1938, the synagogue was burned black, the windows were shattered, and the remains of the books (a Judaica library that was located next to the synagogue and had several thousand precious volumes) were scattered on the sidewalk.

Our school, which wasn't far from there, emerged unscathed from the *Kristallnacht*. Perhaps because of the heavy wood gate that protected it, and maybe because of the nearby Protestant church. Only Moses Mendelssohn's bust, in the little garden, was ravaged by the Nazis' rage. Fragments of the statue were scattered all over the garden, and with it was the shattered concept of emancipation—to be a "German of Jewish faith."

We didn't study at school. Students and teachers sat together, tried to encourage each other, tried to find a solution. That was where I heard that the community was organizing shipments of children to Belgium and Holland. That day, I visited school for the last time, and I never returned to it again. I had more important things to do. About the fates of my forty classmates, I didn't hear a thing.

***

Fifty years later, when I visited East Berlin, I saw the synagogue and the nearby structures standing abandoned, and it seemed as though the stench of fire still stood in the air. A tiny blurry sign indicated that there stood the institutions of the small Jewish community of East Berlin. Dadi and I approached the neglected yard and didn't find a trace of the activity or a living soul we could question.

***

On November 15, 1938, we received notice that our license to hold the store wouldn't be renewed. We had until January first to hand it over to Aryan ownership. If that wasn't enough, the landlord notified us that in three months, our rental agreement would end and, according to the authority's orders, we had to leave our apartment and move to the city center.

Mother, who during all her years of marriage was used to Papa organizing everything, suddenly found herself facing crucial decisions all by herself. For Bronia, who wasn't yet four, we found an arrangement at a Jewish crèche a half hour away by tramcar, and I was in charge of bringing her there in the morning and bringing her back home in the afternoon. On Sunday, on the tramcar, Bronia started crying, and only cried harder when we entered the crèche. When I left, she clung to me, sobbing. When I came back, I found her crying in the corridor, still wearing the coat and hat that she refused to be separated from all day. This repeated itself every day. After a month, we gave up. Bronia stayed at home under eight-year-old Betty's supervision and, once again, became a mischievous, laughing little girl. She would take all the pots out of the kitchen cupboards, draw with colorful pencils all over the wallpapered walls, and smear shoeshine everywhere. Her lovely smile accompanied all of her pranks, and it was hard to get mad at her.

Now Mother gave me an even harder assignment: to collect the debts from the shoemakers. I went to them and found them working in crowded, unventilated rooms, apartments that had the stench of fried pig fat, cheap cigarettes, and mold. Some of them welcomed me kindly, gave me sweets, and told me stories about the good old days before World War I, when the Kaiser Wilhelm ruled Germany, a time when everything was cheap and sons respected their parents. Others were rude to me, as though I had come to beg for alms. They all told me that they were in a bad way and asked that I return in another week; maybe then they'd have money.

When they asked how my father was, I answered that he was ill and that we needed the money to pay for an urgent operation. I had a feeling that if I told them he'd been expelled back to Poland, I wouldn't see a penny. Thus, accompanied by that wretched feeling, I'd go from door to door and beg. I wasn't very successful, but in the end, some of the debts were paid off.

Mother wasn't satisfied. She scolded me and told me I gave up too easily. After closing the shop in the evening, she left to consult with her brother Marcus. I prepared dinner for my two sisters and put them to bed. I locked the door securely with the security chain. I didn't fall asleep until Mother returned late at night. Every noise scared me. On nights like that, I read anything I could put my hands on. I won't forget a scene in Oscar Wilde's book, *The Picture of Dorian Gray,* in which Dorian saw his true face, twisted because of his crimes, his evil, his debauched behavior, while presenting to the world a pleasant, lovable face.

The date to pass the store to Aryan ownership approached, and at the beginning of December, Mother managed to sell it for a couple of hundred marks. She knew the buyer prior to the transaction. He had a small shop on a side street, and he paid pennies for a reputable shop on the main street. Apart from changing the name of the shop, he didn't change a thing. In the sixties, I went with my cousin Gusti, who lived in Berlin after the war, to see the shop. We found the same illuminated sign that Papa had installed above the window display.

It was time to sell the furniture. Mother put an ad in the newspaper, and every day, buyers filled the apartment. Some were just curious to see how the Jews lived. They opened the cupboard doors, passed a rough hand on the polished surfaces that Papa had always been so careful not to scratch. They rubbed their hands over the heavy oak table, sat in the easy chairs, and checked the round table with the engraved copper top. I spent many rainy Sundays in that corner, playing cards with Papa.

The buyers came and left. Mother stated a high price, and those who were interested knew it was only a matter of time until they'd get everything for a token fee. I suspected Mother behaved this way deliberately, because she didn't really want to sell. But eventually, everything that makes a house a home, including paintings, curtains, and rugs, was sold. In one corner, just the bookcase remained, crammed with thick holy books.

Mother stood, her eyes red and swollen from crying, when the porters came to collect the furniture. I told her, "Mother, it's just furniture," and she replied, "Ruthchen, can't you understand that they're taking a slice of my life?" I was ashamed. I wanted to cheer her up, but I only hurt her.

On *Silvester* 1938/9, we drew the shutters of the shop so no one from outside would see a light burning inside, and all night long, we counted, organized, and packed the remaining merchandise. Exactly at midnight, the church bells rang, and cheers for the New Year burst out of the throats of thousands who filled the streets. Fireworks illuminated the sky. In previous years, my parents would wake me up at midnight, open the windows despite the cold, toss chains of colorful papers to the street, and participate in the festivities. Mother would prepare donuts that always turned out dark and greasy, to her and our disappointment. This time, I was afraid that one of the revelers would discover us and break into the shop.

When January first dawned, we closed the shop, which was no longer ours, and moved some of the merchandise to the apartment, things Mother hoped to sell in the future. The "good room," which was empty of furniture, now stored boxes full of shoe polish, rubber soles for shoes, and work tools for shoemakers.

I looked out of the window. The street looked abandoned, covered with dirty remains of colorful paper. Here and there, a drunk wandered about, not finding his way home. In front of our house, a beer-dazed man hugged a streetlight and sang it filthy ditties. Tired, I fell into my bed. I was sad but full of pride that I could be of such help to my mother.

In January 1939, my uncle Marcus, aunt Mali, and their little golden-haired boy, Manfred-Mier, joined their three other children who were in a boarding school in England. My uncle was a Czech citizen, so he didn't need an entry visa. He promised my mother he'd get us entry visas to England. The days passed slowly, yet with a faint hope that Uncle Marcus would manage to help us.

I was the first one who ran out of patience. I thought there was no point sitting around and waiting. "I'll try to expedite my departure from Germany," I said, and I went to the *Eretz Israel* office, which was on the west side of the city, far away from where we lived.

During that month, I came to know Berlin, visiting places I'd never seen before. All the activity of the Zionist movement concentrated in the building of the *Eretz Israel* office, and like every other bureaucratic organization, I was sent from room to room, from bureaucrat to bureaucrat. And yet, the atmosphere was relaxed; young men walked around in shorts and open shirts in the height of winter, greeted each other with a Hebrew "*Shalom*," and called out to each other by their first names. I filled out many forms, and in the end I was invited to a meeting in which I was told that I was too young to join the Youth *Aliyah*, and too old to be included in the group of children immigrants.

"No matter," they said. "In another year, we'll be able to give you a positive reply."

Unhappily, I went to the offices of the Jewish community in Berlin, where I found a different atmosphere. Everything was official and formal. Once again, I wandered through the corridors, searching for someone who would listen to my family's hardships.

An impatient official flung the naked truth in my face. "First, we have to take care of our Jews, the German Jews." And I, where did I belong?

In the building's yard, I met girls my age and found out that they'd received a briefing before leaving for Belgium, some of them to foster families, others to children's homes. Every day, I returned to the courtyard of the building until I had accurate information about the date, hour, and train station from which this group of eighty children would leave for Belgium.

I told Mother my plan. Betty and I would board the train, supposedly on our way to England. During the train journey, we'd join the group of girls and arrive with them in Belgium. It stood to reason that the local community there would take care of us until we'd be reunited, in England. I didn't believe I'd manage to convince Mother to agree to my adventurous plan, but to my surprise, she too assumed that it was our only chance to escape Germany.

We didn't have much time. The following days were full of preparations. After running from office to office, we received documents in our names in which it was written that we were Jews without a citizenship. Everything was ready: train tickets to Belgium and a suitcase full of new clothes that Mother bought. One day before we left, Mother surprised me and also bought me a watch, the pinnacle of my dreams.

TWO GIRLS ON A TRAIN

It was a cold, clear day in February. A weak winter sun stood in the high white sky. Wearing heavy winter coats with matching scarves and wool hats, we walked to the train station. Winter's fresh air was replaced with congested air that never changes. The grayish-white light filtering through the glass ceiling cast a sickly luminescence upon the people.

We stood, silent and freezing. From afar, I noticed a large group of girls saying goodbye to their relatives, standing in threes so it would be easier to count them.

The whistle of the approaching train pierced the air. My throat constricted, and I felt nauseous. Mother hugged us, uttering standard words of farewell, words one said at a train station. I was petrified. I didn't feel the sorrow of our upcoming separation; I didn't cry. I just wanted to board the train and put an end to the nightmarish waiting.

We boarded and found a car in which there were two men

reading their newspapers and an old lady with a ridiculous hat. I had a hard time putting our suitcase in the netting above our seats, but no one bothered to help me, as my black, curly hair revealed my Judaism. I had no choice but to climb on the seat and store the suitcase above us. The woman sitting next to me sent me a hate-filled look. Fifteen minutes later, the train pulled into a West Berlin station.

A figure that looked like our mother ran, waving her hands, until she reached us. "Ruthchen, Betty!" she yelled, and hugged us with all her might.

I don't know how she managed to get to the west station in time to meet us again. Only a mother who sends her children into an unknown future can do that.

The train left the outskirts of Berlin and crossed a snowy open plain. Again, I climbed on my seat, this time to take down the suitcase. I took Betty's hand, and we moved from car to car. Every time we passed from one car to the next, Betty was frightened. When we heard the cheerful chatter of girls, we joined them. I told them we were traveling to England via Brussels and that we'd love to join them. The escorts of the group, wearing the sign of the Red Cross on their sleeves, passed between the compartments, checked the list of names, and secured a tag on every girl's coat lapel.

Time flew as we chattered, and at noon, the train stopped at Cologne, where I found out that it would continue its journey in two more hours. During that break, the girls were invited to lunch at the city's Jewish community center. We got off the train as well, sat on a bench close to our car, and ate the sandwiches

Mother had prepared for us, waiting for the time to pass. Once again, I was gripped by nausea and restlessness. Betty leaned on my shoulder and dozed. I envied her.

Finally, the girls returned and excitedly showed me the presents they had received. While they chattered, the train approached the German-Belgium border. German officers boarded the train, checked the documents I showed them, and left. The train moved, left Germany, and stopped. This time Belgian officers boarded, passed from car to car, and stopped by us. We didn't have the tag the rest of the girls had on their coat lapels, and the officers signaled that we should get off, onto the platform. What should we do? I pointed at one of the chaperones, as though implying that he check the matter with her. Then I grabbed Betty, who was already standing on one of the steps, and sprinted madly through the cars. We had practiced jumping from one car to the other before. The train started moving and we were in Belgium. We returned to our seats. Night had fallen. Here and there, there were glimmers of light in the pitch darkness. Where would we sleep that night? The wheels of the train rattled, and I imagined I could hear its wheels rattle monotonously, "What will we do? What will we do?"

The train stopped again. We'd arrived in Brussels. We got off with the other girls in a city that greeted us with wind and rain. The chaperones called out, "Girls with the red tag, get on the bus to your right. Those with the blue tag, get on the nearby bus." As for us, we didn't have a tag and we couldn't choose. Nevertheless, I chose the closest bus, and after a brief ride, we arrived at an illuminated building with a spacious foyer. On the stairs was a red carpet that led to a large hall, full of men and women who waited for "their girl." I held Betty with one hand, and the suitcase with the other. No one else carried a suitcase.

In the middle of the hall was a small table, and the man standing next to it read names from a list. Name after name, each girl met her adoptive family. Gradually, the hall emptied, and we remained standing, pressed against the wall in a dark corner, with our heavy winter coats and suitcase.

"What are your names? Where did you come from? Who are you assigned to? You're not on the list!" An uproar rose around us. "We have no place for you. You have to go back home!"

I insisted. "We have no home, we have no address, we have no place to return to!"

But they insisted too. They wanted me to give an address. But I stood my ground. "We have no address."

By then only a few people had stayed in the hall, which suddenly seemed so gigantic and scary. They huddled together and whispered in French. I tried to understand what they were saying, and suddenly I heard, "Salvation Army." I understood that they wanted to send us to spend the night at the Salvation Army.

Then, the dam broke and I burst into inconsolable tears. Betty shouted, "No, no, don't send us to the Salvation Army!"

An elegant woman, who was on her way out with a little girl she'd just welcomed, stopped and asked, "What's going on?" After a discussion with the other adults, she turned to us. "Come!" she said. We accompanied her. Was this a dream? A chauffer opened a car door, and I fell into the soft seat. We drove away into the night.

"We're here," the kind lady said, and we saw a villa with bright lights. At the entrance stood a young woman with a tiny white, lace-trimmed apron. Her hair was gathered beneath a small white cap.

"*Madame est servie*," the young woman said, a sentence that I understood from my French lessons. Everything looked as though it were taken out of a movie.

***

The Padawers, our host family, had two sons. One was my age and the other was Betty's age. We all sat around the table: our host, a silent man who was much shorter than his wife, his two sons, the new daughter they had just adopted, and Betty and me. The grandfather also lived with them, but he had already gone to bed and we met him the next day. The table was set with much pomp, including wine glasses and water glasses, knives and forks of every shape and size, fit for each course. The maid, who quickly served the meal, stood behind us, alert to any request.

The food was unfamiliar to us: soup with cheese crumbs on top, all sorts of vegetables such as leek and eggplant, which we had never eaten before, and salads with an oily yellowish seasoning called mayonnaise. Betty, who never was much of an eater, struggled with every course. For dessert, we were served half a *pamplemousse*. Betty saw the yellow fruit and was overjoyed, but then we found out that *pamplemousse* was a bitter grapefruit.

We were extremely disappointed.

The Padawers spoke French, and I tried to remember what little French I learned at school. The eldest son also studied Hebrew, so I used some Hebrew words too. In the morning, I helped with the household chores. I learned to make mayonnaise and all sorts of salads and set the table properly. The family had a factory that made raincoats. It was no wonder that they had a successful business, for in Brussels it rained almost every day.

After two weeks in her house, Mrs. Padawer told us that they found us a place in one of the children's homes owned by the Jewish community in Brussels and she would take us there. After a short drive outside of Brussels, we came upon a flat plain of soaked and grayish earth, and the car stopped before a high brick wall. We entered through a narrow gate and saw a large, wide building of two or three stories, with an expansive, impressive façade. "We've arrived at the Home General Bernheim," Mrs. Padawer said, waved goodbye, and returned to her car.

We were sorry to see her go. Sometimes I wonder what happened to that family. Did they manage to escape in time? Even now, a warm feeling of gratitude fills me when I remember those people, who opened their house and hearts to us, two refugees whom no one wanted, and restored our trust in humankind.

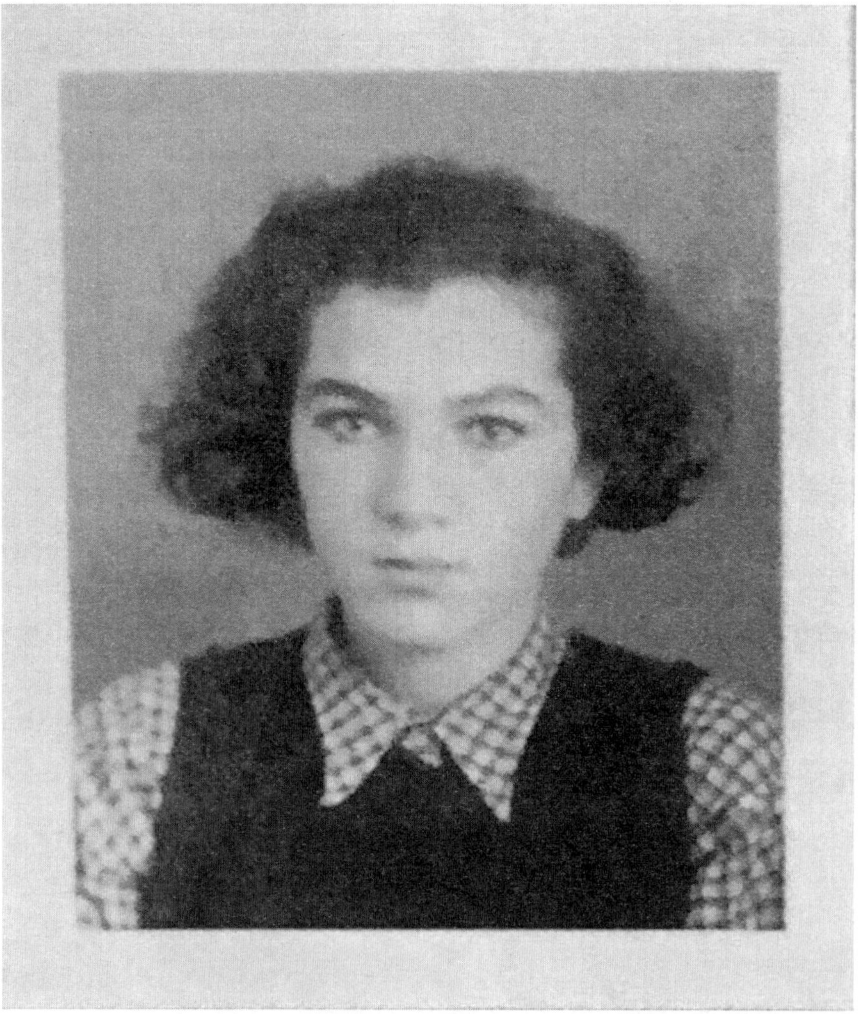

Ruth in Grenoble, 1943.

A JUMP TO LIFE

We stood in a long, narrow, and dark hall, its walls covered with mahogany wood. With one hand, I held Betty's hand; with the other, I held the suitcase. In the middle of the room stood exposed tables, and around them sat girls who examined us with looks that were part curious, part indifferent. Then they returned to eating their bread and jam from overflowing bowls of food. Endless minutes of embarrassment passed until a matronly woman noticed our discomfort, asked us our names, and brought us lukewarm sweetened tea. Madame Schlesinger would be a leading figure in our children's home during all the years of the war.

The Home General Bernheim was hurriedly founded to receive the influx of children who escaped from Nazi Germany. Its managing board, the "Committee," was a voluntary organization of the Jewish community in Brussels and was composed of high-society ladies who accepted the task. Their main concern was providing the children's basic needs: food, hygiene, and healthcare. When we arrived at the children's home, the educational staff there was understaffed, temporary, and unprofessional. The situation improved after the arrival of a couple, Elka and Alex Frank. The Franks were very young and also inexperienced, but full of enthusiasm and devotion.

Days passed without structure or purpose. There simply wasn't anything to do. The girls spent hours sitting on the floor, playing "five stones." I preferred playing dodgeball in the yard when the weather allowed it. I was good at it and was a popular addition to each team. Sometimes, we played from the early morning hours until late into the night.

My entire childhood I lived with Betty, but there, in the children's home, we were separated. Betty was placed in the little girls' wing, while I was put in a large dormitory with the older girls. Meals were the same. There were days I was so busy that I almost forgot Betty. Only when someone harassed her did I become the big protective sister who didn't hesitate to raise a hand at her bullies if necessary.

Betty missed Mother terribly. I missed all the things my parents' home symbolized: the welcoming of the *Shabbat*, the fun-filled holidays, the magical twilight hours on Saturday evenings when we waited for three stars to appear in the sky in order to turn on the light, taking walks with Papa in the park. I missed it, and I knew it was gone, never to return, and there was no point in getting my hopes high.

Mail was distributed at lunchtime, and we waited for it anxiously. When a letter arrived from home, Betty and I were overjoyed, just as we were disappointed when nothing came. Betty was only nine years old, but she was a prodigious and diligent letter writer. Like myself, she clung to the only tie to the world we had lost. Since we had no money, Mother sent us international stamps so we could reply to her letters.

Two events that hurt me terribly were related to that same letter exchange. During our first month at the home, one woman on the staff summoned me and scolded me scathingly. "This is what you write home about? That we don't light candles here on Friday and don't sanctify the *Shabbat*?" I was deeply insulted. I realized my letters had been opened, that my only remaining scrap of privacy had been stolen.

The second embarrassing incident was when two girls found my mother's letter and burst into laughter when they saw her spelling mistakes and the style, which was full of Hebrew and Yiddish expressions.

I've always needed only a few hours of sleep. I used to read in bed until late, but in the children's home, we were forced to turn out the lights early, and I had difficulty falling asleep. One night, when all the girls were asleep and I was dozing lightly, in the dim light, I suddenly saw someone walking across the room, approaching the window, climbing, and trying to open it. I noticed it was a new girl who arrived at the home several days before. She came wearing a straw hat decorated with all sorts of fruit, and her fancy dress was no less ridiculous than her hat. Her hair was strawberry blonde, her face freckled, her blue eyes watery, and her nose big and crooked. Her face and bony body were at complete odds with her attire, and when she told us she excelled at sports and had won diplomas, the girls burst into mocking laughter and started calling her "Dipl"—short for diplomas.

When I saw that girl climbing the window, I tensed, realizing something awful was about to happen. I rushed out of bed, pulled her with all my might, and yelled, "No, Inge, I won't let you jump! Tell me why you'd want to do something like that?"

We sat and talked all night long. The next day, the girls saw us together at mealtime, playing, and everywhere else. A special friendship developed between us, and we kept the details of that night a secret.

***

I found out that in 1942, a group of three girls and two boys, Inge among them, tried crossing the border from France to Switzerland. A German patrol stopped them and took them to the guardroom. Inge managed to jump out of the window and escape; this time she jumped to save her life. The others were sent to Auschwitz. Inge managed to make her way to Switzerland and, after the war, immigrated to the United States.

However, that isn't the end of her story. Decades later, in 1994, I received a phone call from the United States. The caller, a young man who introduced himself as Inge's nephew, asked me to tell him everything I knew about her. He told me Inge was a tragic figure and she suffered from survivor's guilt for abandoning her friends. That guilt haunted her all her life and was the cause of her early death. Years after her demise, her nephew stumbled upon her diary and decided to retrace the story of her life and publish a book in her memory. The book was published in the United States in 2004, under the title *Inge: A Girl's Journey Through Nazi Europe* and was very successful.

After the incident with Inge, I noticed that every girl in the home had her own problems, and they all struggled to adjust to their new reality. I realized that at least I was fortunate enough to grow up in a loving family, something that many girls didn't have, and I stopped feeling sorry for myself.

***

When spring came, a new instructor came to the home. On Fridays, she took us for walks in the area. There was nothing impressive about our surroundings. The area was flat with fenced pastures, small plots growing grain, barley, and rye. A small stream meandered among them lazily, and on the sides of the roads, there were the ramshackle homes of the farmers. Nevertheless, the excursion was a refreshing change.

Wood sorrel with bright yellow flowers grew on the banks of the stream, as did delicate blue bellflowers and sprawling white surfaces of chamomile. The earth was moist, and a strong sweet fragrance rose from it. The instructor taught us to listen to the songbirds and the sounds of the night birds. We walked through stalks of grain and followed their growth—only one week before they'd reached our knees, and the following week, they skimmed our thighs. On our way back, we stopped on a small bridge over the stream and leaned on the railing, and our instructor taught us a new French folk song. There was one song I liked especially. Today, when I translate it, the words seem foolish, but at the time they excited me.

"Listen closely to the fire,
A magical rustle rises from it
These are fiery pieces of wood Whispering in friendship."

Well, it sounded better in French.

Sundays were different. Most girls left to visit relatives, friends, or colleagues. Only a few stayed at the children's home, Betty and I among them. The Franks, who managed the home, asked the women of the Committee to find something for us to do on Sundays. And indeed, one Sunday, at four in the afternoon, a special car came to the home and we were divided among the Committee women. I found myself in a big café, in the company of three well-dressed and well-groomed women, dripping in expensive jewelry. They chattered avidly among themselves, smoked cigarettes, and drank coffee. They ordered ice cream for me. I sat there and didn't know what to do with myself. After some time, they remembered me and ordered another ice cream for me.

The car finally arrived at six and took me back. I returned to the children's home burning with humiliation, while they probably felt elated for doing something good for a little refugee. After another failed attempt the next Sunday, I decided to stay at the children's home.

Shortly after, I found a way to spend my Sundays. The women

of the Committee forbade activity on behalf of any youth movement, but the girls from the Zionist Youth Movement found a way into our children's home, where they taught us French songs and folk dancing. The management was grateful for their activity, which enriched our lives and eased our boredom. One of the instructors, a member of the Bnei Akiva movement, found me an adoptive family (for Sundays) whose son was a member of the movement. Thus, I also started participating in the movement's activities on Sundays, and no one in the children's home knew about it. Fortunately, the first meeting I participated in took place in a forest near Brussels, a celebratory gathering of all the youth movements in Belgium. I experienced the unbelievable and the unforgettable: A sea of blue-and-white flags fluttered in the spring breeze, many youths in their uniform stood at attention, in circles, as they sang, at the top of their lungs, "Hatikvah," the national anthem. I stood among them and sang with them.

***

At the end of August, several days before the German attack on Poland and the outbreak of World War II, my mother came to Brussels with Bronia. Mother was on her way to England—she'd managed to secure a job there as a housekeeper for a crippled old man. Betty and I were overjoyed, and Mother, as usual, brought us a basket full of fruit. I sank my teeth into a big juicy peach, and tears welled in my eyes when I remembered the abundance of summer fruit in our house. Here, in the children's home, I'd almost forgotten the taste of fruit.

I asked Mother what she would do with Bronia since she had no visa for her, and told her I'd heard of incidents in which women who had entrance permits to England to work as housekeepers and tried to pass with a child were unsuccessful, and were sent back. I also told her that many immigrants were wandering hopelessly around Brussels, huddling together in subhuman lodgings, eating only one meal a day in soup kitchens, and trying to pass the time sleeping in order to dull their hunger pangs. "I don't want you to be in that situation!" I told her.

After many deliberations, Mother decided not to endanger her only chance for a better future. We went to talk with the Franks, and agreed that Bronia would stay at the home for a while, with Betty and me, until Mother was able to bring all of us to England.

I walked Mother to the train station, and this time the tables had turned. She stood crying on the train, waving goodbye, while I stood on the platform, ran after the train, and heard her shout, "Ruthchen, take good care of the little one! Good, good care!"

***

Ten years would pass until I'd see Mother again. When I said goodbye, I was a fourteen-year-old girl. The next time we met, I was married, a mother with a one-year-old baby. It was at the Port of Haifa. I stood there, trembling with excitement, and waited, trying to identify Mother from among all the women who stood on the deck. I was afraid I wouldn't recognize her. Perhaps it was that woman with the hat, or maybe it was that one with the light-colored dress? I turned to Dadi, who stood by my side and supported me. Mother, on the deck, nervously surveyed everyone standing on the dock. Suddenly our eyes met and that was that. My mother's luscious black hair was completely white, but her face was the same face, with wrinkles of sorrow and signs of the passing years.

***

When I returned to the children's home, I found Bronia petting a little kitten. Every day, she sat in the corner of the room, petted it, and told it, "My mother went to London and left me here all by myself."

Bronia was four years old, and the home wasn't suited to her age. After a while, she was sent to a Belgian orphanage, far away from Brussels. I asked for her address and begged for permission and the means to visit her. It was the height of winter when I finally succeeded, and I went to see her for several hours. The director called for Bronia, and the sight that greeted my eyes shocked me. Before me stood a withdrawn child, wearing faded clothes, and when she saw me, she clung to me, sobbing bitterly. The director said she was a bad girl who spoke German even though it was forbidden, who wet the bed and had to be punished until she ceased that bad habit. I declared that at home, Bronia was a clean, happy, easy child. But it was to no avail. The manager insisted that Bronia was a bad girl. When we were alone, Bronia told me that she was locked in a dark and tiny room for hours. I don't know if this approach helped her stop wetting the bed, but it was obvious that it scarred her tender soul terribly. Her situation horrified me, and I tried to convince the Committee women to transfer her to another place. The answer I received was, "We'll try, we'll check, we'll see what we can do." In the meantime, precious months passed.

***

At the beginning of the new school year, all the older girls were sent to school. I was sent, with four more girls, to a vocational school where we studied sewing. The Committee women had good intentions; they wanted us to have a profession. The school was in Anderlecht Quarter, an old, poor area in Brussels. The atmosphere was very strict, the teaching methods old-fashioned, and the general level poor. I hated that place from the moment I stepped inside. In the morning, the girls, gathered in a narrow, cold, and damp lobby, had to wait for the principal in complete silence. We would stand there, our heads bowed submissively, as she surveyed the ranks. At her sign, we passed by her, our heads still bowed, and only then were we allowed to raise our heads. This ritual especially angered me, for my father had told me that a Jew never bowed before anyone, only (sometimes) before God. I always tried to situate myself in the middle of the crowded row and pass by the principal with my head held high. Every morning, I feared she'd discover my rebelliousness and kick me out of school. I tried to convince myself that it actually wasn't all that difficult to bow my head like everyone else, but every time, I passed the principal with my head held high.

Our studies were divided between theory and practice: learning various seams and embroideries and preparing patterns. After my mother's death, I found a letter in which I told her about these studies. "I don't enjoy school at all. I don't have the patience or the talent for sewing. Based on the teaching methods here, even talented girls wouldn't be able to make a simple blouse at the end of the school year."

The theoretical lessons were taught to the students by an archaic method. The teacher would write on the blackboard, and the students had to copy everything into their notebooks and memorize everything before the next lesson. Apparently, memorizing and understanding were sometimes two different things. We received our grades according to continuity and speed of the recitation. It so happened that girls forgot part of a sentence and spouted a bunch of unrelated words that sounded like illogical gibberish. We'd giggle, but the girl reciting the lesson usually didn't understand why she didn't receive a good grade. After all, she'd recited the entire chapter!

The teacher placed much importance on what our notebooks looked like. And the notebooks really were lovely. We'd write the names of the chapters with a thick pen nib and the subchapters in inks of different colors. Everything was organized and highlighted, like it was on the blackboard.

The students' seating order was according to grades. The student with the highest grade sat on the first bench in the first row, and so on. After the first semester, we five Jewish refugees sat in the first five places.

Until then, the hostility toward us was verbal. We were called

"*Sale Boshes*," which meant "filthy Germans." Yes, we received abuse for being German! Although we were quick to explain that we weren't Germans, that we loathed the Germans no less than they did, they didn't understand. Sometimes insults weren't enough, and they poured ink over our notebooks and sabotaged our work. Their hatred for the Germans stemmed from the horrors of World War I, during which the Germans invaded Belgium and turned Flanders Fields into a bloody battlefield of death.

We asked for a transfer to another school, and once again received an answer that there were difficulties and our requests would be considered.

Commuting to school took an hour, and there was no point in going home for lunch. Therefore, we spent our lunch hour at the orphanage Home Speyer, where the Jewish refugee boys were sent to. A room was cleared for us at the edge of the yard, which the boys were forbidden to enter. However, sometimes a boy would pass by to get a look at the girls. The room where we ate our lunch wasn't heated, and we found an original way not to freeze: by singing and dancing. This just piqued the boys' curiosity. We couldn't know that within several months, our fates would be intertwined.

***

May 10, 1940. An interminable dull rumbling woke me up. The windowpanes shook, creating a clear, high sound, as though they were screaming in fear. I jumped out of bed to see what had happened and froze in place when I saw flashes of light and heard explosions that were replaced with an eerie, expectant silence. The sirens wailed, a long, nerve-wracking sound.

Planes bombed Brussels. The Nazi regiments had invaded Holland and Belgium. The Wehrmacht marched down the roads, and the skies filled with the white parachutes of German paratroopers. The atmosphere was one of fear and terror.

In the dining room at dawn, the Schlesingers and Elka Frank, a young woman in her twenties, sat surrounded by many frightened girls. From the home's single radio, we heard inconsistent announcements and instructions. Obviously, Belgium was at war. Elka Frank, whose husband Alex had been drafted into the Belgian Army, was solely responsible for fifty girls. All day long, as well as the next day, she tried to contact the Committee women, but to no avail.

For years, we'd thought that the Committee women had abandoned us, but recently, documents were found indicating that they were well aware of their responsibilities and that they feared for the fate of the young people under their supervision. They'd truly tried to find a solution. Following the death of one of the women, Mrs. Feldiger, dozens of letters that she wrote to the U.S authorities, appealing to them to open their gates to all the children, were discovered. The women also managed to collect a considerable sum for the matter. Eventually, they managed to send sixteen children to the U.S. with the help of a Quaker Christian organization. But the children could enter only if they had relatives in the United States.

Masses of terrified Belgians fled south to France, and the roads were full of people and various vehicles. Elka Frank thought Belgium would have to surrender in several days and went to her brother-in-law, a high official in the government, for help. Two days later, we were ordered to leave the children's home within a matter of hours, and each of us was allowed to take only a small bundle.

I ran in panic to the nearby telephone in a desperate attempt to call Bronia's orphanage. All the lines were down. I told Elka I couldn't leave without finding my sister first. Somehow, she managed to convince me that Bronia was being evacuated as well. I collected my most precious possessions: a photo album and amber necklace I received from Papa. I also took my toiletries bag. One of the girls suggested we wear layers of clothes, and we followed her advice. We left wearing several pairs of underwear, a skirt over a skirt, shirts, and woolen clothes. Unfortunately, we could wear only one pair of shoes. Then we walked clumsily and heavily to the train station.

Brussels' train station was packed with people who were fleeing to France. We managed to shove into that human knot and huddled together on the floor. We sat there for hours, from the early morning hours, and no one even knew if and when a train would arrive. Elka Frank gave each child two dry cookies, and I remember eating them slowly. I wasn't really hungry since, just that morning, Elka had opened the storeroom and we all devoured chocolates and sweets. The first day of the war is associated with that pleasure, of eating as many sweets as we wanted. Come evening, before darkness fell, we heard the whistle of the train as it entered the station.

Elka's brother-in-law managed to secure two cars ahead of time, one for us and one for the boys from the Home Speyer orphanage. These were cars to transport animals on which was written "For ten horses." The doors closed, and only a narrow opening let in some light and air.

The train started moving slowly, and in the darkness, I searched for Betty and made a place for her next to me. We both fell asleep on the crowded floor, curled up like fetuses, and that's how we traveled for six days. Once every so often, the train slowed down for no obvious reason and sometimes stopped. We had no food, but fortunately, the boys brought with them loaves of bread and shared with us. Sometimes, when the train pulled into one of the stations, we received a cup of soup from women wearing the sign of the Red Cross.

We shouted, "Long live France!" and from the platform, people answered, "Long live Belgium!"

One day the train stopped to allow the passage of a train that came from the other direction. We were shocked to see cars filled with the wounded, lying on stretchers, their entire bodies bandaged. These were British soldiers who were injured in France and on their way home to England. Some of them started singing "It's a Long Way to Tipperary," and we joined them.

In one place, German bombers bombed the train and hit the last car, where a group of nuns sat.

We passed through France from north to south, without seeing any of its views or cities, and then, one evening, we arrived at a remote town, about thirty kilometers from Toulouse. All the children were invited to the town hall, and the mayor welcomed us with a flowery speech. Once again, we heard "Long live France!" and "Long live Belgium!" and were served soup. That evening, we were taken to a nearby village, where we were brought to a building with a floor covered with straw. We fumbled around in the dark, peeled off layers of our clothes, took off our shoes with a sigh of relief, and fell asleep.

UNCLE GASPAR'S REGIME

The next day, we were told we were in a village named Seyre, in the region of Haute Garonne. The village was small, with several low houses, some of them abandoned, and a dirt road that led to a small church with an adjacent cemetery. In the local post office, two old ladies sat and sold tobacco and sweets. Many of the village's youngsters left long before the war, and the remaining men were drafted into the army. The only people left were the old ones and the village madman. Ironically, he's the only one I remember. He always walked around with the same rancid, ragged clothes and a faded hat. When he'd see one of us, he would burst out in a roar.

The view wasn't especially magnificent: cornfields and, here and there, neglected fruit trees. Low hills covered the horizon and created a claustrophobic feeling, as opposed to the open plains of Flanders that we'd grown used to. Dry prickly weeds covered fallow land, and the vegetation wasn't green and juicy like it was in Belgium.

We were about ninety boys and girls from the ages of seven to seventeen, and six administrators and caretakers—Elka Frank, a young Flemish caretaker called Leah, the Schlesingers, and "Uncle Gaspar" and "Aunt Louise," who managed the boys' orphanage in Brussels. We were put in filthy, derelict structures full of cobwebs and without any furnishings or dishes. Two structures were used as dormitories, one for the boys and one for the girls. The French government allotted aid for the Belgian refugees, and the administrators used what we received to buy the necessary equipment.

Food was short: Morning and evening, we ate corn flour porridge, sometimes sweet, sometimes seasoned with onions, and at noon we ate soup from intestines, pork fat, and a kind of turnip that looked like a potato, which smelled and tasted revolting. The food wasn't fit for human consumption. During the first weeks, we didn't even have benches and ate standing up. A pump on the street provided water for us. Once a week, we heated water on a bonfire, bathed, and then washed our clothes in the same water. The girls had it easier, since we wore several layers when we left Brussels. The boys didn't even have a change of underwear because they left with only the clothes they were wearing.

Before long, most of us were sick with diseases that stemmed from malnutrition or poor hygiene. I had festering sores in my mouth and had a hard time eating what little food we had. At night, I lay awake on the straw and breathed in the cold air to somewhat ease the pain. I also had sores on my arms and legs, and at night, the straw poked the wounds and the pain became unbearable. Since the straw wasn't changed, the festering infection spread among the girls. Elka Frank took good care of us and smeared the open sores with ointment. I examined my arms and legs, full of blue scars, and asked myself if these ugly scars would remain with me for the rest of my life.

In addition to the sores, we were plagued by lice. Every evening, the older girls groomed the children's heads with combs dipped in kerosene, yet the next day, a new generation of lice would hatch from the eggs that stubbornly clung to their hair. In the end, there was no choice, and crying and begging didn't help. Everyone had their hair shorn. We were no longer girls with curls or braids. After the haircut, I found Betty crying, curled into herself. Her shorn head was one big wound, oozing puss from the lice that had dug paths and tunnels in her scalp. She wanted some solace from me, but I only said, "If we'd cut your hair in time, you wouldn't have reached this state." I kept up a tough façade in order not to show my sister how horrified I was by the state of her head.

***

At the end of June 1940, France surrendered and was divided in two. The north side was occupied by the Germans, while the south side was under so-called French rule headed by Marshal Petain, a senile old man who was under the Germans' thumb and carried out their orders. Suddenly our remote village was full of French soldiers who no longer had any military action to perform. From them, we heard about great France's shameful defeat. The soldiers who wandered around the village were restless and unruly, and it wasn't long before they started harassing the girls terribly. At night, we boarded the doors and the windows with planks, and when we managed to fall asleep in spite of the heat and the suffocating conditions, the soldiers, who tried to break into our dormitories, woke us up with their drunken singing.

But the toughest thing was the regime of terror imposed by Uncle Gaspar. I don't know on account of what skills he and his wife were chosen to manage the boys' orphanage in Brussels. Uncle Gaspar was a Christian Belgian in his thirties. He was skinny and pale with thinning blond hair. His face was round, the lenses of his glasses thick, and his thin lips were permanently pursed. He looked like a meek minor official in a government office. He never greeted us with a "Good morning," and he never exchanged a word with any of the children. But he fastidiously maintained order.

Three times a day he'd stand at the entrance to the dining room and supervise the children who stood quietly in threes. Among us, there were very young children. We all wore clumsy, noisy wooden shoes; therefore, long minutes would pass until Gaspar was satisfied and signaled that we were allowed to go in and sit on the wooden benches. Then he'd instruct us to straighten our backs and cross our arms behind us. He wouldn't let us eat until there was complete silence.

Every child had to eat everything on his or her plate, and at the end of the meal, we were to wipe our plates with a slice of bread, as the French did. My stomach revolted against the smell of the broth, in which pieces of pork floated. I would search for a child willing to receive my food the minute Uncle Gaspar turned his back.

We were punished for every transgression, even the slightest one. Gaspar would approach silently and then would roar and catch the culprit, for example a child who spoke in German. We called him "the Panther" on account of his silent footsteps and his patience when stalking the culprits.

Betty, who was ten, listened once in amazement to one of the children and absentmindedly exclaimed "*was*" ("what") in German. Her punishment was a week of confinement in a room while subsisting only on bread and water. I worried about her because she was so skinny, so I found a way to pass more food to her; I asked Uncle Gaspar for permission to give part of my meal to his dog, whom I loved, and when he agreed, I ran off to bring the food to Betty. That's how that week passed somehow.

In October that year, Belgian refugees were allowed to return to their country. Gaspar and his wife, who arrived like us, without a thing, left the village with two overflowing wagons, full of goods they bought with the money they saved from working with us. They left without saying goodbye, and we were glad to get rid of them. Alex Frank, who until then had served in the Belgian Army, was discharged. He came to us, and from then on, he managed things with his wife, Elka.

Here's the place to tell you about this wonderful young couple. Elka was born in Berlin, a daughter of the extremely religious and wealthy Bart family. The Barts arrived in Israel shortly after Hitler's rise to power and founded a candy factory that still exists today. Alex, an agronomist born in Belgium, grew up in an assimilated family, and after his studies, he traveled to Palestine. Elka and Alex met in Kibbutz Ein Harod, where they got married. They weren't Zionists; they were communists. They left Israel and settled in Brussels, where they managed the home for girls.

Alex, who was strong with a tough face, believed in abstinence and was strict with himself and with others. We accepted his toughness because we appreciated his honesty and dedication. Obviously, Elka's life with him wasn't easy. She was an ordinary-looking young woman, not pretty and not ugly, her face soft and babyish. She had an overbite, she lisped slightly, and her demeanor conveyed insecurity.

In Elka's and Alex's hands, everything ran peacefully. They knew how to care for and educate, under lacking conditions, ninety boys and girls without punishing any of them.

Our lives started assuming some order. The older children were responsible for the younger ones and escorted them from the moment they woke up until the evening. I was in charge of a group of girls, aged ten to thirteen, and I tried to teach them what little I learned myself, without any textbooks or guidance. In the afternoon, we'd organize games, and in the evening, we taught songs and dances. It wasn't long before we discovered talents among us. Heinz came with his violin. Walter, who was the oldest in years and spirit, was also a musician. Out of nowhere, we conjured a piano, and the two of them played together all day long. That was how we learned to enjoy Mozart and Schubert and other classical music.

Frieda decorated the bare walls of the dining room with the

images of Snow White and the Seven Dwarves from the Walt Disney movie. Fifty years later, when Alex Frank visited the remote village, he discovered that only four families remained out of all its wartime occupants, but Frieda's paintings were still in the abandoned barn.

***

The lack of food was extremely difficult. Madame Schlesinger cooked vegetable soup from nettles, so we'd go out to pick them. "If you grip the nettle tightly, the leaves won't burn you," Alex told us, and we picked them and tried to ignore the pain. At the end of summer, the fruit on the blackberry bushes growing on the side of the road ripened, and we received a refreshing addition to our meager meals. We raided the cornfields, hoping to find cobs that remained after the harvest, and I was reminded of Ruth the Moabite and the laws of the Torah that said to leave leftover harvest for the poor and needy. This custom wasn't known to the French farmers, who meticulously picked every cob of corn from the field.

Not far from the village, there was a chestnut forest. At the beginning of November, we started collecting chestnuts. The air was chilly, and moisture rose from the rain-soaked ground. No one but us was in the area. The isolation added magic to the situation. At noon, we lit a bonfire and warmed ourselves, roasted some of the chestnuts in the embers, and ate. The rest we took back to the village and cooked for dinner. Each child received a rationed portion of chestnuts, which we ate in the dark, and this way we could get some animal protein (the worms in the nuts).

We also made jam with the chestnuts and saved it for special occasions. One of the boys couldn't resist the temptation. We caught him one night licking that sweetness, and he was shunned and ridiculed so badly that he left us. I have no idea what happened to him. He never tried to contact any of us. That was the power of a group of children under siege: extremely cruel collective discipline.

The winter of 1940–1941 was especially hard. The freezing cold caught us unprepared. We had no appropriate clothes, shoes, or bedding. Each child had a blanket of rough wool, which we called a "horse blanket." We huddled together in threes and covered ourselves with three blankets. We wore wooden clogs and wrapped our feet in newspapers. In the morning, I'd break the layer of ice in the water tank and make sure the girls I was in charge of washed their faces and hands. There was no heating in our structures, and only the soup served at lunch defrosted our frozen hands.

One day, I had a high fever, and when I was served the daily corn porridge, I felt terribly sick. Many of us were infected with hepatitis. I don't remember much, only that I actually wanted to die. I lay ill for many days, perhaps weeks, and I remember that eventually, one cold and clear day, I sat outside, trying to catch rays of the winter sun. I took a deep breath of clear air and said to myself, *It's good to be alive.* I had recovered from my illness. Later, when I saw the movie *Miracle in Milan*, in which there was a scene with the residents of the shantytown standing close together, stamping their feet, and trying to get warm under the rays of sun shining through the clouds, I remembered that day that I returned to life.

***

It wasn't the harsh conditions that weighed on me, nor the food shortage, nor the cold, nor the diseases. These were hardships that we all suffered from. I was haunted by my concern for Bronia. I didn't know what had happened to her. Mrs. Frank's assumption was proven false, and according to the news I managed to gather, the children of the orphanage where Bronia had been staying never made it to France.

I was in agony, for Mother left me in charge of her and I promised I'd take care of her. There were mail connections with England, letters that took weeks but eventually arrived. I corresponded with Mother, but I lacked the courage to tell her that Bronia wasn't with us and that I didn't even know where she was. Every letter Mother sent started with "How's the little one?" and I would write that the little one was growing up and everyone loved her. What else could I do? I wrote to the Swiss Red Cross and asked them to help me locate her. After several long months, an answer arrived, and I found out that Bronia was in a Jewish orphanage in Brussels. It was only then that I wrote the truth to my mother.

After many years, I read *Promise at Dawn* by Romain Gary, which was about a young French pilot who served in North Africa. His mother sent him letters regularly, and only when he returned home after the war ended did he find out that she succumbed to a disease. However, before her death, she wrote several letters and made sure he'd receive them. When I read the book, it touched me, and I thought that perhaps I'd been right to spare my mother and not tell her the truth.

***

That wasn't the end of Bronia's story. In 1942, when she was just seven years old, she was sent with the rest of the children of the orphanage to the Malines camp in Belgium. From there, most of the children were later sent to a death camp. According to one version, one of the English officers, who was a prisoner of war, grew extremely attached to little Bronia, and he managed to smuggle her to the Bal family. According to another version, it was the members of the Belgian Résistance who managed to find a way to smuggle some of the children out of the camp and bring them to families who wanted to foster the persecuted young ones.

Bronia was welcomed with open arms by the lovely Bal family, who lived in the little town of Sint-Niklaas, and suddenly she had a *Paps* and *Maps* ("Mother" and "Father" in Flemish), an older brother and sister, a spacious house with a garden, a dog, and a cat. From then on, she was called Brigitte, and the Bals introduced her as a distant relative so as not to arouse suspicion. Bronia forgot Papa's home in Berlin. She forgot German. The only things she remembered were that her real name was Bronia and she had a mother in London and two sisters named Ruth and Betty. With that scant knowledge, the Bals went to the Red Cross and managed to contact us when Belgium was liberated.

When the war ended, Henri Bal traveled to London to meet my mother. He wanted to make sure he was leaving his beloved adopted child in good hands. For Bronia, it was once again a painful separation. Mother and Betty were strangers to her, as was the culture of poor, anxious, orthodox Jewish immigrants.

It was 1955 by the time I finally managed to see my sister. Bronia was twenty years old and wore thick-lensed glasses. It was hard for me to see in her the mischievous four-year-old I'd remembered. One evening, Betty, Bronia, and I left a concert in Albert Hall. We were in high spirits, when Bronia suddenly cut off the conversation and said, "Maybe I'm not really your sister?"

That sentence contained the entire tragedy of her childhood. She didn't have any shared memories with us. She felt isolated and foreign, and even with Mother, she never established a real closeness. Perhaps she was angry that she'd been torn away from her beloved home in Belgium. And as for Mother, I always felt she secretly resented me for convincing her at the time to leave Bronia in Brussels at the children's home.

***

I wasn't used to boys my age. The only boys I knew were my cousins: Yaakov, my aunt Chache's son (my father's sister), and Sigmund, Uncle Marcus's son. They both left Germany in 1938, when I was thirteen. In Seyre we lived together, boys and girls, from morning until evening. We shared our entire lives, but nevertheless, that fact didn't diminish the awkwardness I felt in the company of the opposite sex. I was reserved.

One day, when I drew water from the village well, Werner, one of the bigger boys, approached me and, on a "tray" of leaves, served me shiny blackberries he'd just picked. "I picked them for you," he said, and then added breathlessly, "I'd really like to be your boyfriend."

Werner was a handsome youth, seventeen years old, with long, straight light-brown hair, which frequently flopped on his forehead and was swept aside with a graceful movement of his head. "Boyfriend? What does that mean?" I asked him.

The next day, he invited me to join the daily meeting where they organized the group's activities and daily routine. He was a rationalistic young man, talented, ambitious, and arrogant. He was well versed in French, and under his tutelage, I wrote the meetings' protocols with German precision. I had to state the time the meeting had begun, the time it ended, the names of those present, and more.

We would walk hand in hand, roaming the area, discussing religion and other important matters. I already felt that my faith in God was weakening, and I no longer observed the commandments. I wasn't in love with Werner, but my friendship with him instilled in me self-confidence and opened new horizons and a different world view. In 1941, he finally received his much-hoped-for visa and traveled to the United States. We tried to kiss goodbye, and I felt ridiculous, like I was in the scene of a Hollywood movie.

***

Seven years later, when I lived in Israel, in the midst of the War of Independence, I received a letter from Werner. Enclosed was a picture of him as an American soldier.

I wondered how he managed to get my address. In the letter, he wrote that he was serving in Germany as a military censor, that he'd changed his name to one that sounded more American, and that he'd adjusted happily to the American way of life. He didn't mention his parents, who'd been murdered in the Holocaust, didn't write about his feelings for the Germans, and didn't express any concern for our welfare in a country that was embroiled in a ruthless struggle. I didn't bother answering his letter, and we lost touch. Werner didn't keep in touch with any of the "graduates" of the children's home, and none of us heard from him. We assumed that he probably managed to move forward in life to the best of his abilities and ambitions.

Many years passed, and in September 1997, I received a letter from him, out of the blue. Here's a brief summary:

Dear Ruth,

We haven't been in touch for more than fifty years. First let me ask for your forgiveness and try to explain why I disappeared and why I decided to write to you.

Shortly after I arrived in the United States as a very young man, I decided to leave the horrifying past behind me and embark on a new life. I changed my name from Werner Rindsberg to Walter Reed.

It's hard for me to judge whether this was the right decision, but it allowed me to live a good, successful life.

In August this year (1997), when I was seventy-three years old, I traveled with my wife and two sons to France. I had a burning desire to visit the places where we lived: Seyre and La Hille.

I cannot describe to you the excitement I experienced when I learned about the fates of my friends from La Hille. I told my family about you, "my first love," and was profoundly affected when I found out about the events in your life and your bravery in those distant days.

Following the visit, I told my wife and sons, for the very first time, that my family had died in the Holocaust. My parents and two younger brothers were sent in March 1942 from my home town in Germany to the Lublin Ghetto in Poland, and only recently have I received information concerning their fates through Yad Vashem.

I arrived in the United States in 1941. In 1943, I was drafted into the army and served, among other things, in the intelligence service department in Germany as an interrogator of war criminals. I was discharged in 1946 and studied journalism and international relations.

I'll thank you if you respond to my letter, tell me about your life in Israel, and send my warm regards to the "children" of La Hille whom you still keep in touch with.

In friendship and love,
Yours, Walter.

Since then, Walter's life changed completely. He started to dedicate most of his time, energy, talent, and quite a lot of his money to commemorate the Holocaust in various frameworks. Among other things, he initiated two reunions of the La Hille children. The first was a one-day reunion in the United States, and the second was in 2000, in the city of Toulouse, and lasted for four days. La Hille children from all over the world participated in it. They visited the villages where they spent a portion of their childhood and reminisced. The visit prompted a powerful reaction among the village people and local media.

Walter kept in touch with all the survivors, and every year, he publishes a newsletter containing news about all the surviving "children" of La Hille. He also plans on publishing a book about the orphanage. This frenzied activity done at such an old age can be understood as a sort of compensation for years of ignoring and isolating himself from the past.

***

In 1941, Belgian citizens returned to their countries, and the French government stopped sending us the stipend we had received until then. The situation became dire. There was nothing with which to buy necessary products for ninety children. Fortunately, Mrs. Goldschmidt, one of the Committee women in Brussels, remembered us and managed, thanks to her husband's ties with the Red Cross, to involve Maurice Dubois, who was in charge of the organization *Secour Suisse Aux Enfants*, which was affiliated with the Swiss Red Cross. The couple examined our living accommodations and decided to find us a more appropriate place in which they would establish a children's house under their patronage.

Château de La Hille, undated.

CHÂTEAU DE LA HILLE

At the beginning of 1941, a pioneering group of youths went to Château de La Hille to prepare the place for us. The castle had stood abandoned for dozens of years. Therefore, all the rooms were in dire need of cleaning, the plumbing had to be repaired, and electricity had to be installed. In March, we all moved to the château, which was about thirty kilometers from the ancient city of Foix, near the Pyrenees Mountains.

I was charmed by the surrounding view and the château's romantic visage. It was a real castle, with a heavy, impressive gate that led to an inner courtyard, with two side towers and walls covered with ivy. The dining room floor was made of wood tiles. Green hills surrounded us, and a stream bubbled nearby, its water as pure as crystal. The air was clear and intoxicating, and plane and cypress trees contributed to the beauty of the landscape.

In the dormitory, we found a bed for every child and two good blankets. From Switzerland, there was a shipment of powdered milk and chunks of yellow cheese sliced for Sunday's breakfast. Every Thursday, we received an egg with our corn porridge. Unfortunately, Alex Frank decided we had to eat the egg raw so that it would maintain its entire nutritional value.

In May, Mademoiselle Naef arrived at the castle, and from that moment on, she was in charge. She was tall and blonde, with wide shoulders. She was approximately thirty years old, unmarried, her hair brushed back fastidiously, her attire lacking color and ornaments as befitting her job. She was diligent, energetic, practical, and tough. She had no patience for emotions and soft feelings and didn't want to listen to the hardship of her young charges.

Rösli Naef brought with her boxes full of things contributed by Swiss citizens. There were thick plaid cotton textiles, from which we sewed dresses for each girl. At night, the girls and boys wore a stiff gown of natural linen, which apparently served generations of Swiss farmers. The sight of grown boys wearing short, wide embroidered gowns reduced us to tears of mirth. Boxes of books arrived, most of them filled with old textbooks: chemistry, physics, math, and history.

Ms. Naef made sure we wouldn't have any free time. Her motto was "Idle hands are of the devil." The boys worked for the farmers in the area, and the girls were in charge of cleaning the house, doing the laundry, helping in the kitchen, and taking care of the vegetable garden. We grew cabbage, carrots, lettuce, and radishes. As for reading, Ms. Naef didn't allow anyone to open a book during the day. If one of us was caught committing such a sin, she immediately found them something to do.

Before long, a group started rising before dawn to read the textbooks, before the official wake-up call. The pages of those books were yellow and stained and gave out a faint smell of dust and mold, but we didn't care. I read about the French chemist Lavoisier, an eighteenth-century scientist who discovered the role oxygen played in combustion. For the first time, I learned about atoms, molecules, and the laws of chemical reactions. I was sorry I couldn't repeat the experiments described in the book. We sat there, boys and girls, each with his or her head in a book in the predawn gloom, fascinated by what we were reading despite the cold and the uncomfortable seating arrangements on the hard wood benches.

In the summer, another member of staff joined Ms. Naef—Eugen Lyrer. He was a Christian Swiss, a forty-something-year-old bachelor, of medium height. He was quiet, reserved, with thin black hair and a melancholic expression. He spent most of his time in his room alone. Lyrer taught us English, French literature, and German shorthand. I didn't see much point in German shorthand, but I participated in the lessons because that was what we had.

The main thing was that Eugen Lyrer was a man of the book. He traveled to Toulouse and bought books for us there, perhaps with his own money, and after several months, our library contained approximately one hundred novels. Assisted by a dictionary, I read all of *Les Misérables* by Victor Hugo. There were chapters that were extremely tedious because of the archaic style and the flowery language, but it was worth the effort, and from then on, I could enjoy reading fluently in French.

In the library, we also had books by Romain Rolland (including all the volumes of *Jean-Christophe*), the saga *The Thibaults* by Martin du Gard, which I especially loved and copied entire pages from, books by Anatole France, George Sand, Jules Verne, and *Treasure Island* by Stevenson. There were also poetry books by Rimbaud, Verlaine, and of course, Baudelaire, and classics by Racine and Corneille, and plays by Molière. To my joy, I was chosen to be the librarian and helped the children find books according to taste and age. There wasn't a book I hadn't read in our library.

In the evening, we crowded around Monsieur Lyrer, who read chapters from books he'd chosen to us. He had a quiet voice, and it was pleasant listening to him. We looked forward to the evening so we could listen to the adventures of *The Mother* by Gorky, the hardships of the man from *The Death Ship* by Traven, or the stories of the English Brontë sisters. We enthusiastically put on plays, mostly by Molière, such as *The Misanthrope*, *Tartuffe*, and *The Imaginary Invalid*. Walter and Heinz continued playing and performing concerts. Sometimes Ilse sang the songs of Schubert and they accompanied her.

Alex Frank's mother also came to stay at the château. She was a very tall, skinny woman, with a bird's head covered with tiny silver curls. To us, she seemed at least one hundred years old. She was passionate about philosophers' quotes, and every morning before we ate the watery corn porridge, she welcomed us with a quote by one of her much-admired philosophers—Pascal, Descartes, or Rousseau. The morning joke was "Montaigne said . . ." (I forget the rest), and only after the quote ended would we hear the "*bon appétit*." It can be said that, thanks to Lyrer's and Alex Frank's mother's contributions, that year was rich with culture.

When the crops matured in the fields, a clumsy threshing machine appeared out of nowhere, attached to a tractor. During the threshing season, the machine passed from farmer to farmer, and a regular group, mostly young men, moved with the machine from farm to farm. The workers gathered the sheaves from the field, piled them next to the threshing machine, and lifted them to a platform, where two girls stood and fed the sheaves into the machine.

The workday began before dawn and ended when darkness fell. In these areas, the days were long in the summer, and darkness fell after ten in the evening. In the morning, the farmer's wife would prepare hard-boiled eggs, butter, bread, homemade salty white cheese, and jars full of sour wine diluted with water. When the work ended, there was a real feast, with baked chicken, roasted rabbits, and pork chops.

The farms were quite a distance from each other. Except for Sunday, during which they went to pray in church and then to the tavern, the farmers lived an isolated life, each at their own farm, with their families and animals. Only the threshing season in the summer and pig slaughtering in the winter were periods of social gathering and events.

I was among the few girls of La Hille who worked during the threshing season. I stood all day long on the platform and quickly fed the sheaves into the machine. The dust, the sweat, and the sun burned my eyes. My hands were covered with blisters, and my feet became heavy from standing in one place all day long. I was grateful for every one of the machine's mishaps, which allowed us to rest a bit.

While we worked and broke our backs, the mechanic lay in the shade, combed and clean, ogled the girls, and conveyed arrogance and derision toward the hardworking farmers. When there was a mishap, his honor would get up, swagger importantly to the machine, and fix it.

That was the first time I learned to recognize the abysmal difference and contempt that existed between city folks and farmers.

When darkness fell and the workday was over, all the workers would gather around rough wooden tables, and as they drank wine and ate meat, they'd ogle the girls. It wasn't long before the young men would start fighting over the girls and throw punches, to the glee and encouragement of those sitting around the table. This happened every evening. I felt foreign to the situation and tried to excuse myself as early as possible. I didn't touch the meat anyway, and the crude chewing and wild behavior disgusted me. I couldn't eat nonkosher meat, not then and not now.

The village girls married at a very young age, and at the age of thirty, they already had several children and had been through many miscarriages. With their black, long, faded dresses, they looked old long before their time, and at forty, they looked ageless, like the rest of the village's old women. The villagers didn't bathe often. They claimed it was hazardous to their health and mocked us for our bathing habits. One time, I mustered my courage and asked one of the women how they managed without sanitary pads during their periods. To my amazement, she didn't even understand my question. They didn't wear underwear at all, and the blood poured down their legs beneath the black dresses.

During the threshing, I came across the farmers' cabins. Some of them didn't even have windows, and only a hatch in the middle of the ceiling let in some light and air. The floors were made of concrete or packed earth, and along the wall, in a slightly elevated area, there was a place to light an open fire with a chimney over that. On the ceiling, there was a hook and a chain on which they hung the pots: a large pot to cook food for the pigs and a smaller one to cook for the household members. The menu wasn't varied; most of them cooked bean stew with pork fat and meat, sometimes potato soup.

In the winter, when there wasn't any work except taking care of the animals and preparing wood for heating, the household members would sit for hours and hours and stare at the fire as they warmed their feet. Sometimes they'd separate the corn from the cob, and sometimes they'd just sit idly, or get into bed. The adults spoke the local dialect, which was similar to Spanish.

Once, one of the peasant women asked me where I was from, and when I said I was Jewish, she startled, crossed herself twice, and felt my head to see if I had horns. In the end, she said it was impossible, because I looked just like any other human being, and it couldn't be that I was a spawn of the murderers of Jesus, the son of God. Even in places where there were no Jews, Christianity spread hatred against them. This is something that still exists, even in places where Jewish communities have been annihilated.

Nineteen forty-one ended. We were isolated in a remote part of the country, and we knew very little about what was happening in the world. Our only source of information was a one-page newspaper the size of a notebook page, which the Vichy government published under Nazi patronage. We knew that the Nazis had invaded all the European countries except England. The British fought, and their cities were being bombed horrifically. I also knew that Germany started a massive attack on the Soviet Union and advanced rapidly into the country. Matters that year were dire, and there wasn't much hope.

I was terribly worried about Mother, who lived in bombed London. Later, she told me that during the Blitz, while she worked in a uniform factory, she wouldn't leave her workstation despite the sirens, and she didn't go to the bomb shelter with the rest of the workers. When they urged her to come with them, she said, "I have nothing to lose, and I'd better continue contributing to the war effort."

After the war, my mother received British citizenship and became an enthusiastic English patriot and a great fan of the royal family.

***

The management of the La Hille children's home passed to the hands of a Swiss team. Alex Frank left; he joined de Gaulle's army and then the British Air Force. His wife and mother left with him. We celebrated August first, the National Swiss Holiday, around bonfires and put on a play about the adventures of their national hero, William Tell.

At Christmas, we really strayed from the dreariness of our lives: We decorated a fir tree with glass balls, glittery tinsel, and angels with glowing wings brought from Switzerland. In the evening, we ate the chestnut jam we'd kept. Mrs. Schlesinger prepared a hot, filling dish from bread, sugar, and milk powder, which we called bread pudding. The recipe was local, and I haven't eaten it since, but I still remember how satisfying it was. At night, in the corner of the dormitory, the fir tree stood, its candles bright. I tried to stay awake in my bed and fully absorb the warmth and festivity that I missed so. I dimly remembered Saturday nights at my parents' home.

At the same time, Ms. Naef's discipline grew worse, and she imposed new, strict Swiss rules. Every morning, she checked the angles of the folded blankets, and on the door, she hung a piece of paper on which she stated the achievements of each child in precise folding and similar tasks. I was sixteen, the world was on fire, I was worried about my parents' welfare, the future was threatening and uncertain, and our director treated us as though we were mentally challenged children. I felt terribly insulted. I rebelled, and in a rage one day, I tore the list from the door. The conflict between Ms. Naef and myself lasted several weeks and became unbearable.

Ruth and her sister Betty at Château de La Hille, 1942.

THE GREAT CHASE

In the end, I found a solution. I found out that the Schmutzs, a family of Swiss farmers with a farm that was a two-hour walk from La Hille, were looking for a maid. I hastily offered myself for the position without even meeting my employers, and that same week I left the château. Betty was devastated I was leaving, and I consoled her and promised to visit as frequently as possible. I packed my few possessions and started walking toward the hills, some of them still covered with snow. I walked from hill to hill without meeting a living soul or seeing a house on the way. After an hour and a half, I reached a road that led to Tambouret village and from there to the yard of the Schmutz's farm.

I received a warm welcome in that humble house, which mainly consisted of one central room where the family cooked, ate, and spent the evening hours. In addition, there were small bedchambers. In the middle of the main room stood a big table on an earthpacked floor, and in the corner stood an oven. From the ceiling hung glue straps full of trapped flies, and the walls were splattered with black spots, probably marks that the flies left before they were trapped. The father of the family, a man in his fifties with a sunburned face, was stocky, with shoulders that slumped forward from constantly walking behind a plow. His wife was short and thin, her face wizened, her eyes kind and determined. She created a laid-back atmosphere, which I sensed the moment I arrived.

The boys, Hans and Rudi, were in their twenties and looked like giants. They were tall, wide, and heavy, half of their bodies stuck in huge boots. When I saw them wearing undershirts, which exposed gigantic, muscular arms, I thought Samson the Great must have had arms like that when he'd destroyed the gates of Gaza. The two large brothers scared me at first, but it wasn't long before I learned they were kind-hearted and friendly.

In the evening, they showed me my room—a niche in the wall with a bed covered with a comforter stuffed with goose feathers, and a checkered pillow case. A little ladder was attached to the bed so I could reach it, and I also had a kerosene lamp at my disposal. A corner that was just mine—a dream come true.

I slept late the first morning. Mother Schmutz had already prepared the regular breakfast meal: *röschti*—thick potato fritters cooked the day before, grated, and then fried in oil. This was hours after the men of the family had left for work in the dairy farm and in the fields. I felt uncomfortable, and Mother

Schmutz, noticing my unease, calmed me and said, "You slept well, so you'll have enough strength to work properly."

That was her approach. She never rushed me, and even when I failed to fulfill an unfamiliar task, she instructed me kindly and encouraged me. I tried, I really tried, to be useful.

The family had a large farm, more than 200 *dunams*. On some of it, they grew grain and corn, and the rest was used for pasture. They had thirty milking cows and two oxen for plowing. The vegetable garden was the women's responsibility. We grew lettuce, carrots, radishes, cauliflower, beans, peas, and potatoes. In the yard, there were fruit trees, and hens ran around, laying eggs in hiding places, which we later had to search for. There was a lot of work: preparing the meals, taking care of the vegetable garden, the hens, and the geese, washing jars of milk, and more. I helped bring the cows back from the pasture, made cheese, and churned butter.

When darkness fell, after we finished milking the cows and the day's work came to an end, Mother Schmutz would take out old Swiss annuals and weeklies. We'd gather around the kerosene lamp and browse through them until exhaustion defeated us. On the clear summer evenings, we sat outside and saved kerosene. Sometimes the boys played the harmonica and Father Schmutz would yodel along, as per Swiss custom.

On Sundays, Hans and Rudi would brush their teeth, wash their necks and feet in a bowl that during the rest of the week served as a salad bowl, and put on clean shirts and pants that I laundered and ironed with a coal iron. Then, riding their bicycles, they left for the neighboring town. Mother

Schmutz would claim proudly, "We're different from the French. We're clean!" In the evening, the boys would return to milk the cows.

On Sundays, if the weather was fine, I would visit La Hille, a two-hour walk in each direction. One day, when they returned from town, the boys brought me a pair of sandals as a gift, the first new personal item given to me since I left home apart from the wooden clogs and cotton robes we received at the children's home. The sandals were very fashionable, with cork heels (since there was a shortage of leather) and blue textile straps. They weren't appropriate for working on the farm or for walking down the rocky road to La Hille, but they made me so happy, and I hoped that one day I'd be able to wear them.

During all the months I lived with the Schmutz family, I never heard them raise their voices at each other, nor did I notice signs of impatience or complaint. They spoke sparingly, contented themselves with little, and were happy with their lot. They didn't have visitors, and the war was a distant thought as far as they were concerned. Their circle of life was small and safe and contained the fields, animals, and house.

On Christmas 1943, when I was a member of the Résistance, I received, to my surprise, a postcard with a picture of a fancy lady in the arms of a slick, polished man. On the other side, in French, were the words "I love you and want to marry you." It was signed "Rudi." Apparently love bloomed slowly with Rudi. I had no idea how he found out my name and address. Probably through Eugen Lyrer from La Hille. At the time, I changed my name frequently, and my address also changed regularly. I didn't reply. How could I even respond to such a declaration of love?

***

In the last week of August 1942, at noon, I returned with a basket of fresh vegetables from the garden. From afar, I noticed a black car parked in front of the house and two brawny men wearing the black uniform of the French militia standing next to it. I froze in place and took a deep breath. I had a flashback of the black car and the SS men wearing black uniforms who took my father in Berlin four years ago.

They addressed me. "Is your name Ruth Schütz?"

"Yes, that's my name."

"We have a warrant for your arrest. You have five minutes to collect your stuff."

Mother Schmutz stood by the oven, raised her head for a second, and then returned to her business. They were simple people, and as far as they were concerned, the authorities were always right.

I asked, "What did I do and where are you taking me?"

They answered, "To a labor camp. It's about time you Yids work!"

I wanted to say, "But I am working," but their demeanor was threatening. I remained silent.

Several minutes later, I stood with my bundle in my hands. The officers went through my stuff, checking to see if I had hidden scissors, a knife, or a razor. And if that weren't enough, they then checked to make sure I hadn't hidden a weapon on my person. I was filled with rage. "You think that I want to kill myself?" I protested insolently.

They kicked me into the car, and Mother Schmutz managed to push a paper bag with food for the journey into my hand.

After half an hour, the car stopped before the police station in the town of Pamiers. Without another word, I was put into a holding cell, a heavy door closed on me, and I found myself in a tiny room with a barred window looking out to the street. It was a clear, nice summer day, and from the window I saw women and men, wearing city clothes, probably clerks, hurrying home for lunch. Children rode around on bicycles, and groups of young men and women passed by chattering and laughing loudly. I also saw a pair of lovers—a girl in a flowery dress and a young man lowering his head to her. More than two years had passed since I'd seen well-dressed people and young people having some carefree fun. Apparently, it still existed in the world, but I had no part in it. I asked myself if I was cursed. Outside, girls my age were strolling about, so why was I locked behind bars?

In the evening, I was taken to a car already containing a family—parents and their two little children sitting on their laps. They didn't respond to my greeting and remained withdrawn. We traveled a short distance until we reached the gates of the Vernet concentration camp. A long line extended in front of a table in the middle of the concourse, and a clerk registered the men, women, and children rounded up that day from the area.

In the camp, there were rows of long barracks, and it was

surrounded by an electric fence and watchtowers. In every barrack, there were forty two-tier benches adjacent to the wall, and from the ceiling hung one lamp that gave off a dim light and burned all night long.

How could I even notify someone that I'd been arrested and was in the camp? I couldn't sleep. The light, the guards' footsteps, the rustling made by so many women who, like myself, couldn't rest on those benches, chased sleep away.

Early in the morning, there was a census, and every woman was required to stand next to her bench. For breakfast, they weighed a sticky lump of black bread for every person and gave us something brown and murky to drink. The man who gave out the food, a dark skinny man with curly black hair, saw I had no bowl for the beverage. "You didn't bring any utensils with you?" he asked.

At lunch, just as they started distributing the food, I procured a bowl. Ramon—that was the name of the Spaniard who was one of the veteran detainees—found an old food tin and made me a bowl with a handle and a rounded rim, as well as a tin spoon. "You have to clean the tin carefully after every meal. Clean it in the sand, which is everywhere," he guided me.

That day, the head of our barracks passed through the rows of women and asked, "Who has nice handwriting? I need help." And the next day, I had a job. I sat in his room and compiled long lists of the prisoners.

At first, Camp de Vernet was a prison for criminal offenders. Later, it held political prisoners, mainly Spaniards who had fled Franco's regime. And in the end, it served as a detention camp for Jews. There were three sections in the camp, each one for a certain category of prisoners. In order to move from one section to the next, one needed the guards' permission. The camp's population was varied, and contained mainly men. Women and children were held only in the Jewish section. The head of my barrack was a Belgian who received regular packages from his wife. In the evening, he'd boil tea on a small burner and share the cookies she sent him with me.

Among the prisoners, there was a handsome Brazilian who stood out. He was in charge of the food distribution and always walked around wearing fashionable, colorful clothes and two-toned leather shoes. In the camp, they called him "Alimente," which meant "he who feeds people." He was involved in everything, and I thought he looked like a pimp.

On the first day, Ramon came looking for me and said, "Do you know how long it's been since I saw a woman or a child?" He told me he was twenty-seven years old, was married, and had a child. He was part of the anarchist faction who fought Franco, and he mentioned that his wife could no longer stand the long years of separation and was in a relationship with another man.

The next day, he managed to visit again and brought with him a harmonica. He played and sang Catalonian songs. When we said goodbye, he asked me to walk with him, and then he stopped among the barracks and hugged and kissed me. Suddenly, a searchlight illuminated the area, and the guard noticed Ramon. He hit him with the butt of his rifle and sent him back to his section in the camp. That's how I remember my first kiss from a man tied to the detention center and the tragic fate of those resisting Franco's regime in Spain.

The French policemen did their job efficiently, and every day dozens of Jews arrived at the camp. I had a routine: get up early in the morning, roll call, stand in line for bread and drink, compile lists, stand in line again for the lunch soup, stand by the faucet that provided water only two hours a day. When I managed to wash something, I'd stay by the rope and wait for the garment to dry. Otherwise, someone would steal it.

The Germans confiscated most of the cars in the area, and the farmers couldn't bring their produce to the market. The surplus of fruit arrived at the camp: half-rotten watermelons, melons, plums, and pears. As a result, the detainees suffered from an outbreak of diarrhea. I remember relieving myself in the latrines, without any privacy, as an extremely humiliating situation.

By the time all the girls and boys of La Hille who were older than sixteen arrived at Vernet, I felt experienced in the ways of the camp. They told me that ten policemen had surrounded the château in the early morning hours, and at dawn, they barged inside and arrested everyone despite Ms. Naef's protests. She shouted, "The children are my responsibility and are under the protection of the Swiss Red Cross!"

Although I was upset they'd been arrested as well, I was happy to be reunited with my friends.

On the morning of September 1, 1942, we felt something strange in the air. The roll call took place later than usual. The camp commander entered the barracks escorted by policemen and shouted out, “All prisoners must pack their belongings and stand by their bunks. When your name is called, go to the train.”

The train tracks crossed the camp, and cattle cars stood, ready to receive the masses. The policemen read name after name, and I tensely waited for them to call my name. Finally, the only two girls left in the barracks were myself and another young woman who’d managed at the time to marry a Frenchman and waited for her release. The guards disappeared without another word, and I wondered what I should do. I went to the barrack where the La Hille children stayed and found them full of excitement. Their names hadn’t been called either, and they were told that soon they’d be released.

Around the train there was chaos. Old men and women lugged heavy suitcases, babies cried, and in this pandemonium, parents searched for their children and belongings. We tried to help those poor people carry their luggage and calm the children. Among them, there were people I’d managed to befriend and heard of their hardships, including those who’d experienced the trauma of the journey on the *St. Louis*, a ship which left the port of Hamburg in Germany and set sail to Cuba. Nine hundred and thirty Jews were on that ship. They’d tried to save themselves, but when they reached Havana, they weren’t allowed to disembark because their entrance visas weren’t valid. When they appealed to the United States, it wouldn’t receive them either. The ship continued to sail until mid-July, when finally, England, Belgium, and France agreed to give them asylum. Now, they’d reached the end of their journey.

We remained there, on the platform, and suddenly I felt I’d

had enough, that I no longer desired to fight for my right to live. And just for a fleeting moment, I considered boarding that train and letting my fate be like the fate of all those Jews. I didn't do that. I returned with my friends from La Hille to the abandoned barracks, where items that the deported had left behind were scattered all around. We wandered there, as silent as ghosts.

The next day, all the children of La Hille were released. Ms. Naef came and took care of the transportation, and we returned with her to the château. Before that, when I went with all my friends to the gate of the camp, Alimente the Brazilian caught up with me and gave me a small object. "A souvenir from Ramon," he said. It was a brooch shaped like an airplane, made of a tin can, decorated with tiny pieces of colored glass. On the other side of the barbed-wire fence, where the political prisoners were held, I noticed Ramon, desperately waving his hands and crying.

I guarded that brooch zealously, as though it was my lucky charm, but in the course of my extensive wanderings, I lost it, which saddened me greatly.

When we approached La Hille, the children greeted us joyously and with a song. Betty was ecstatic with happiness. She jumped on me and hugged me. But I couldn't connect to that joy. I couldn't forget those heart-wrenching scenes I had witnessed just the day before. According to the BBC, which we secretly listened to in Nadal's room (he was our Spanish janitor), those people were murdered while still on the train. From that day, we realized we were mere mortals.

***

It was only many years later that I discovered the circumstances of our release from Camp Vernet. This is what happened: Immediately after the children of La Hille were arrested, Ms. Naef traveled to Toulouse, to the "Secour Swiss" branch there headed by Maurice Dubois. One of the organization's activities was hosting French children, casualties of the war, for several months in tranquil Switzerland. Mr. Dubois acted quickly. He traveled to Vichy, where Petain's government sat, tried to make his way to the Ministry of the Interior, and persisted until he managed to meet with Prime Minister Laval. He demanded from Laval that he release all the children of La Hille and threatened to cut off all assistance to the children of France if he wouldn't acquiesce to his request.

Laval complied, and that evening, he issued an order that we be released, twelve hours before the camp was evacuated and the detainees were sent east. Concurrently, Dubois' wife traveled to Bern to meet the Swiss prime minister and requested entrance permits for all the Jewish children under the organization's protection, claiming that they were in mortal peril. Her request was denied. Eleven La Hille children were murdered during those horror-filled years.

Maurice Dubois saved our lives, but in doing so, he had overstepped his authority and acted against government instructions. Dubois was found incompetent and was dismissed from his high position. Ms. Naef also lost her job. Disappointed, she left the country and lived the rest of her life in Switzerland.

***

In 1990, on a clear winter day in Jerusalem, Mr. Dubois, who was more than eighty years old, planted a tree in the Garden of the Righteous in Yad Vashem. More than fifteen of the La Hille children were present, and after planting the tree, we gathered for a ceremony at which he received a certificate of recognition. I will never forget his words. "Everything I did," he emphasized, "would've been for nothing if not for the courage you had shown, your resourcefulness, and your ability to cope with the most difficult situations, to overcome them yet not lose your faith in humanity. I thank you."

***

Life supposedly returned to normal in La Hille, but in fact, everything was different. We were anxious and felt that the château was a trap, that at any minute, they could come and arrest us again. Miracles happened only once. We made various plans as to how we would escape. I returned for a while to the Schmutz family, whose tranquility was at complete odds with my own state of mind. Several days later, I received an order from the police to return immediately to La Hille. We were now restricted to "compulsory living quarters," and leaving was forbidden. In fact, I was pretty happy to return to the château and be with the rest of the children.

After some time, I was surprised to receive a letter from Ramon. On the envelope, large letters stated that the letter had been censored, and strips of paper were glued to the sides where the envelope had been opened. This fiery love letter embarrassed me greatly. I could imagine the censors eagerly reading the letter while adding their own juicy comments. Ramon's prose was pompous and flowery, extremely different from the stammering French I heard from him in the camp. I had a suspicion that he wasn't the one who wrote it, but rather his slick friend Alimente, a man well versed in matters of love. I assumed Ramon told him what to write, and Alimente revised and rewrote, perhaps with the help of the men in his barracks.

In his letter, Ramon urged me to contact his anarchist friends in Lyon, who would provide for me. He also wrote that I could wait there until his release. I answered that we lived from day to day, that the future was unsure, and that there was no point in making plans. If there came a day when we'd be emancipated from the Germans' regime of horror, I'd want to live among my people and help build a new nation in Israel. Of course, I phrased my letter carefully so that it would pass the censor safely.

***

On November 11, 1942, the Allied Forces landed in North Africa. With their arrival came the end of the Vichy regime. From then, all of France was under German occupation. The Gestapo invaded every city and district and started rounding up young French men and sending them to labor camps in Germany. The Jews were under strict surveillance, and it was clear to us that the interference of the Red Cross wouldn't save us again. In December, the first group of five boys and girls left La Hille for another children's home near the French-Swiss border that was also under the Swiss Red Cross's protection. The plan was to cross the border, and the first group indeed succeeded with the help of one of the women working at La Hille. Several days later, another group left and also crossed the border successfully. One of the members of that group was Peter Salz, who later became a member of Kibbutz Lehavot HaBashan, as I did. Ruth Klonover, who later on became my sister-in-law, was also among those who managed to cross the border.

Encouraged by the success of the previous groups, a third group embarked on the journey. I was supposed to be part of that group, but that night I felt ill and feared that I wouldn't be able to keep up with the rest of the group as they stole across the border, thus endangering them. I stayed at La Hille, and another girl took my place.

The next day, after that group left La Hille, three French gendarmes arrived at the château on bicycles and called out the names of the children who'd left the evening before. We told them, "They must've left for work and will return in the evening. We saw them at breakfast."

The gendarmes shouted at us, "You're a bunch of filthy liars. These people were caught yesterday at the Swiss border, and the Germans have them! We'll be back in the afternoon. When everyone returns from work with the farmers, we'll have a roll call and see who left without permission."

From the group of five who were captured, only Inge survived after jumping out of the window of the guardroom. She hid all day and night, and managed to cross the border by herself. After the war, she immigrated to the United States. The four other boys and girls were murdered at a death camp.

Lixie, a good friend of mine, and I decided it was time to run away. Ms. Naef wasn't at the home that day, so we approached Eugen Lyrer, who had saved for me the money my mother had managed to send a year previously. Lyrer gave us French money, bread, cheese from the emergency stockroom, and also an address in Lyon for someone who would help us arrive safely in Switzerland. We said our goodbyes hastily and left.

***

The last day of 1942 was also Lixie's and my last day at the château. After lunch (corn porridge seasoned with onion), we stole away from La Hille and made our way to the closest train station in Pamiers, a town about fifteen kilometers from La Hille. It was the height of winter. The sky was gray, covered with heavy clouds. We hurried to reach Pamiers before darkness fell. I was familiar with the roads of the area, thanks to my job with the Schmutz family. We walked from hill to hill until we reached the road. It was empty of vehicles and people, but suddenly we saw two gendarmes riding a motorbike and surveying the area. Had they already discovered we had run away? Were they searching for us? We didn't hesitate as we threw ourselves down the side of the road, into a ditch full of mud and melting snow.

We continued. Once again, the motorbikes appeared, probably

a patrol of other gendarmes. Again, we jumped into the ditch. Luckily, by the time we arrived at the train station, it was dark and no one noticed our wet and dirty clothes. We hurried to clean ourselves, trying to assume the regular appearance of two girls going to spend Christmas in Toulouse.

The Children of Chateau de La Hille.
Ruth is in the second row, fourth person from the left.

ON THE ROAD IN OCCUPIED FRANCE

Two hours later, the train brought us to Toulouse. We planned to continue directly to Lyon. "Sorry," the clerk at the Toulouse train station said. "The train to Lyon left an hour ago, and the next train to Lyon is tomorrow evening."

We looked around. All the passengers who'd gotten off the train with us had scattered quickly. The waiting room was empty, the station was dark and empty, and at the edge of the platform, we could see a faint light coming out of the guard's room. What could we do? Where would we find shelter until the next day? Should we spend the night in the station's waiting room? No, that was the last thing we needed to do. We knew that waiting rooms were dangerous. Staying there would arouse suspicions, and we didn't have any kind of identification papers. Therefore, we decided to follow the last passengers leaving the station and see where they would lead us.

Suddenly, out of the gloom, we came across a hotel sign that was illuminated by a tiny torch. We walked inside and said to the clerk at the reception, "We're students. We just missed our train home, and we're looking for a room for the night." "Papers, please," the clerk said.

"We have no identification papers, because we aren't sixteen yet."

The clerk studied Lixie and me. Lixie was blonde, slender, and short. She gave off a childish innocence. As for me, I had a head full of dark curls, I was taller, my body was curvaceous and very feminine, and I looked older than my age. It was hard to believe I hadn't celebrated my sixteenth birthday yet.

"No, we have no vacancies," the clerk said.

"Where can we find a hotel in the area?" I asked.

The clerk went to the door and pointed down the street. "Hurry! The curfew has begun, and it's dangerous to wander outside."

So that was the reason all the train passengers had scattered so quickly. Indeed, the streets were empty. Only a group of German soldiers marched down the street, their boots echoing ominously. We held our breath and pressed against the wall. After they passed by, we continued fumbling along, staying close to the walls of the houses. Suddenly, we arrived at a square in which circus caravans that had arrived in town for Christmas were scattered. We found an opening in the barbed-wire fence and stealthily approached the closest caravan. We climbed several stairs and tried to open the door. Suddenly it swung open and a man, clad only in underwear, stood there.

"Damn thieves!" he shouted, brandishing a thick stick.

Panicked, we ran across the square and found ourselves in

the street again, hoping to find an unlocked door of one of the houses but to no avail. In the end, we saw a very large gate that was open, and we crouched behind it, sheltered from the wild wind. The church bells rang twelve times, signaling that 1943 had begun. The hours passed slowly; it was freezing cold, we were uncomfortable, and sleeping was out of the question. Had I frozen to death? It seemed as though all my senses had abandoned me. Suddenly Lixie shook me. "Ruth, my leg got lost. Help me find it!" I burst into laughter, which helped us regain lucidity and brought us back to reality.

That long night finally came to an end. We got up, tidied ourselves, combed our hair, and tried to straighten our wrinkled clothes. A door closed, and a woman walked down the stairs.

Lixie approached her and asked, "Excuse me, where's the nearest church?"

Once again, we told her our story of students on their way to their families in Lyon, and she was touched. The people of the south were warm and hospitable.

We happily made our way up to her apartment and were served a hot drink with homemade sweet bread. And the most important thing was that we hurriedly used the toilet. As a sign of our appreciation, we gave the woman a tin of sardines from the La Hille emergency stockroom, a precious gift that she accepted gratefully. We felt rejuvenated as we left her house and emerged into the cold, clear morning. We still had to wait many hours before the evening train to Lyon would arrive.

We decided to go to the nearest church, the one whose bells accompanied us during that long night. We entered its dim interior through a heavy wood gate. Some light filtered through the colorful windows in the ceiling, and the smell of incense made me a bit dizzy. Women passed by, dipped their fingers in the basin of holy water, and crossed themselves. Lixie quickly did the same, and I imitated her hesitantly. At a distance, over the altar, was a large painting of Jesus, his head hanging, his wounds oozing blood. The women kneeled before him and so did we. The cold stone floor made me shiver.

A feeling of yearning filled me when I remembered the synagogue in Berlin, which was heated in the winter, its floor covered with a red carpet, the clear light that filtered through the windows, the Holy Ark covered with a gold-embroidered curtain, the two lions guarding it. It was my first time in a Catholic church. While I was deep in thought, Lixie elbowed me in the ribs. "Ruth, the priest is coming to collect donations. What should I put in the box, the cheese or the button?"

"For God's sake, of course the button. Leave the cheese for us."

I trembled with mirth when I heard the button hit the bottom of the box and saw the priest standing before me. I lowered my head and made an effort not to laugh. What was he thinking? Perhaps he thought that the girl before him was praying in anguish?

When the prayers came to an end, we left with everyone else and roamed about aimlessly. The streets were full of German soldiers. The Gestapo headquarters was in the city center. We passed by. The front of the building, along the sidewalk, was fenced in by double barbed wire. Soldiers held submachine guns, their fingers on the triggers, ready to shoot lethal fire into the crowd.

We turned into the side streets of the old city and were surprised to see that the sewer flowed along the sidewalks and housewives emptied their wastewater indiscriminately from the balconies straight to the street. To our surprise, among that filth, dressed-up girls wearing French fashion walked jauntily on platform heels—whether from cork or wood—on their way to enjoy the day. We ran away from the vile smell to the spacious boulevards and stopped before a cinema. German soldiers stood there, checking the papers of the moviegoers. We waited for them to leave, bought tickets, and sprawled in our seats in order to get some rest. After a while, we left to avoid the check at the exit and arrived at the train station early.

The train entered the station with a high whistle, spreading black smoke. Hordes of people rushed to the cars, yelling, pushing, and hitting. Young men climbed the train and leaped through the windows. I was afraid that I'd lose Lixie in the commotion. But she managed to board the train before me, noticed me, reached out, and pulled me up. The train started moving. We stood all night pressed together in the crowd, and I remember leaning against the window, staring outside at the dark night.

As we approached Lyon, I repeated to myself the address Eugen Lyrer had given us—22 Lantern Street. A priest lived there who was supposed to lead us to a guide who would help us cross the border to Switzerland. I thought the name of the street sounded odd. Who'd ever heard of a street called Lantern? And how would we find the priest? We didn't even know his name. German officers passing through the cars and checking documents jerked me out of my thought. Thanks to the crowded conditions, we managed to avoid them, and with first light, we arrived at Lyon.

It was very cold that morning, and we could barely see the houses through the mist. It was too early to go to Lantern Street and meet the priest. Across the station we saw a café, with the waiter taking the chairs off the tables. We sat at one round table and ordered a cup of coffee. It was a bitter beverage, made of acorns. With it, the waiter served a bottle full of a murky substance, which was a substitute for sugar. Of the provisions Mr. Lyrer gave us, very little was left: several slices of dry bread, a few slices of cheese, and a bar of chocolate. In La Hille we were isolated, and we didn't know that we needed ration cards to buy food.

We found the house on Lantern Street easily. The door there was open. We entered a long, narrow room, with walls filled with files and a desk with piles of paper. A middle-aged woman greeted us and asked us how she could be of help.

We told her the purpose of our visit and were terribly disappointed when she told us that the priest had left on a long vacation and she didn't know when he'd return. We stood there silently, and just as we made to leave, the woman returned to her desk, opened a drawer, and took out ration cards. "At noon, go to The House of Christian Fellowship, show them these stamps, and you'll get hot soup," she explained.

And that was that. Gone was our chance to find our contact. We were in a strange city, without any identification papers or money. We left and took advantage of the following hours to check churches and choose one where we would spend the night.

When we arrived at The House of Christian Fellowship, we found people already sitting at rough wood tables, hunched over their bowls. Next to the window sat two young men who looked familiar. They also saw us and approached us, full of excitement. They were Bertrand and Charles, two of the older boys from La Hille who had arrived in Lyon a few days earlier. They told us there was no point in trying to cross the Swiss border because the Swiss government had decided to grant asylum only to pregnant women and children. The rest of the Jewish refugees who arrived there at the same time were sent back to France, and many were captured by Germans, who patrolled along the border. They also told us that they went to a Jewish-French charity, received from it some money, and rented a room in Lyon. They offered to let us spend the night at their room and suggested that we come close to curfew and try to sneak in without anyone seeing us.

The room was small, and there was only one double bed. We lay there, five people—the four of us and redheaded Frieda, who had arrived in Lyon the previous day. We were very careful not to make any noise, to remain inconspicuous.

The next day, before noon, Lixie and I went to the Jewish charity with the hope of receiving some money and advice, but when we entered the building and started climbing the stairs to the first floor, we heard shouting and cursing in German. We hastily hid beneath the stairwell, and from there, we witnessed a terrible sight. The Jewish employees of the charity came down, their hands on their heads, as German soldiers shoved them with their rifle butts. After that, we heard shouting outside and the noise of cars driving away. Silence fell, but it was a while until we dared come out. We were silent witnesses to the end of the Jewish organization in Lyon, and our chances of getting its help were gone.

Every day, we scoured the local papers, hoping to find an ad that workers were needed for farm work. Every day, we returned to The House of Christian Fellowship to receive our daily meal of soup. The soup was thin, made of cabbage or pumpkin or turnips, and it was the only thing we ate. Bertrand and Charles couldn't stand the hunger any longer and decided to return to La Hille. I begged them, "Don't return to the château. Spring will come soon enough, and the farmers will need workers in the fields. We'll make it somehow."

But they were adamant. They returned, were arrested by the French police, were sent to a detention camp and then east, where they were killed. We lost Bertrand, with his shy smile and small, alert eyes, who, because of his short stature, we called Bebe, although his behavior was so mature. He had a quick mind and was beloved by all. And Charles, tall and handsome, always meticulously dressed, his hair perfectly combed, generous, with perfect manners.

How did we arrive at the convent that was on the other side of Lyon, beyond the Rhone River, on a forested hill? Who sent us there? How did we find the way, and what did we say when we knocked on the hidden little door in the narrow alley? I try to dredge the details from my memory, but the only thing I remember is fragmented pictures and scraps of information. Perhaps the harsh despair of those days, the endless existential worry of finding food and a place to spend the night, avoiding the checks for papers, are what caused this obliviousness.

The convent that received us was a little two-story house, which was wonderfully well-kept. Several nuns lived there, walking silently along the halls. The Mother Superior, a woman in her forties, had a broad, open face, and welcomed us kindly. Apparently, there were other refugee girls who the nuns had taken in, and all together, we were ten girls. During all three meals, we sat around a long, fancy mahogany table, and before every meal, we stood, our heads lowered, our fingers folded, as Mother Superior blessed the food. It was a blessing of thanks for our Lord above for our daily bread. In her prayer, she never mentioned Jesus the Messiah, the son of God, and would say instead, "There is one God for all of us."

Starved, I also willingly blessed the food.

The next day, I heard laughter and was surprised to discover girls my age wearing nun's habits running around and playing ball. Slowly, I put together what I'd heard and seen and realized the unfamiliar way of life I'd come across by chance. These girls were students, novices, who were preparing for that great day when they'd pledge their allegiance to their Lord and Savior Jesus Christ. They still had three more years during which they had to blindly listen to their superiors and isolate themselves completely from their families. They took with them nothing from the outside world that could remind them of their past. They even had to forget their names. It was as though they were reborn, receiving a name of one of the saints. And one day, if they endured all the hardships and were found worthy, they would become "Brides of Jesus."

I wondered what caused these young and vivacious girls to choose this way of life and then learned that among French aristocracy, there was an ancient tradition, according to which one of the girls in the family dedicated her life to the Church. As for the poor, it was a way to escape a life of poverty and humiliation and ensure an honest existence for their entire lives.

On the second floor of the house was a "Holy Room" that we were forbidden to enter. I was curious to know what this holiness meant. One day, I had an opportunity to find out. The door wasn't locked, no one saw me, so I entered and peeked at the inner sanctum, which was well lit and bright thanks to the high and wide windows. There were tables, shelves, and dressers full of little colorful statues kept under glass covers, similar to those in which cheese was presented in grocery stores. There were statues of Madonna with the holy baby, statues of saints and angels. I left quickly after deciding I'd seen enough, and I could barely stifle my laughter. What was so holy about those kitschy statues?

The days were long. The only thing that kept us busy was knitting socks from thin wool for charity.

One night, we heard rough pounding on the door.

"Who's there?" Mother Superior asked.

"Open up! Gestapo! You're hiding Jews!" was the answer.

The Mother Superior was a wise, brave, and determined woman. "No man will cross this threshold. This is a convent of nuns!" she said decisively. Words were exchanged, we heard some curses, and the Germans left.

Early the next morning, we left the convent, full of gratitude for what they did for us. How long were we there? Days or weeks? I don't remember. I'm sure I managed to knit only one sock. I didn't have time to complete the second one.

What exactly happened next? Who suggested that the three of us continue to Annecy and what for? Who were we supposed to meet there? Who gave us money for the journey, and how did we travel? I have no answers to these questions, for my memory betrays me.

Annecy, a beautiful town, lies on Lake Annecy, surrounded by the Alps. But we weren't there because of its beauty. I remember that on our first day there, we worked in a big house. The furniture in the rooms was covered with dust covers, cobwebs covered its ceilings, and its floors were made of wood tiles. We polished the windows, cleaned the cobwebs, and scrubbed the wood floor. In the evening, the proprietress gave us soup and, after giving us a few coins for our hard work, got rid of us.

It was getting late, and curfew was approaching quickly. We wandered the cold, empty streets, searching for the nearest church. A priest saw us and, without asking any questions, directed us to a certain address. I've forgotten the name of the landlady and street, but I do remember the spacious house on the outskirts of town and the large proprietress who spent many hours of the day in her bed. The oldest daughter took care of her many brothers and sisters, the older children took care of the younger ones, and chaos reigned. We fit right into the pandemonium, taking huge pots of soup off the burners and distributing a bowl to each child. In the attic hid several men, and the oldest daughter would bring them their food. The children's father, a doctor, wasn't present. There were hints that he had joined de Gaulle, who had established the Free France government in London.

Once again, Lixie, Frieda, and I found ourselves on the road.

This time, we walked most of the way and made our way to a convent by the Swiss border. We walked for several hours and saw that the snowy plains were sparsely populated with farmers' houses. Who sent us to that convent? What was the name of the place, and what order did it belong to? All this is erased from my memory, and neither Lixie nor Frieda remember. It's as though an invisible hand moved us from place to place, like pieces on a chessboard. Was it Luciole (firefly), a member of the Jewish scouts, who contacted us in Lyon? And perhaps it was the initiative of the Mother Superior, who followed the instructions of the renowned Father Glasberg? It's all shrouded in fog nowadays.

The convent we arrived at was very different from the one in Lyon. Here, we heard no talking or playing, no singing, and God forbid, no laughter. Here, most of the nuns took the vow of silence. The walls of the big house were thick and bare, and a statue of the tortured Jesus Christ and big steel crosses could be seen everywhere. The furniture was coarse, the floors were bare, and there wasn't even one colorful item in sight. The nuns wore stern expressions, their faces and shapes ageless. They wore habits of coarse cotton both during the summer and harsh winter. After they showed us our sleeping arrangements, they left us alone.

It was freezing cold there. The meals we received were meager at best and didn't satisfy us. But harder to bear than the cold permeating our bones and the gnawing hunger was the boredom. I'd lie in bed under the thin woolen blanket until noon, desperately trying to conserve some of the warmth my body had generated. One day, I mustered my courage and asked the nun in charge of the library to lend me a book. I read *The Life of St. Theresa* and another book about some other saint, and then gave up on reading too. Those books didn't interest me in the least, and they couldn't break my boredom.

The sink we used to brush our teeth and wash our hands was in the corridor, open to drafts. How would I bathe and maintain a semblance of cleanliness? Thank God for the tin can left over from Camp de Vernet. There, it held food, and here, I washed with it. I filled the bowl with cold water and ran to the bathroom, and after washing myself, I'd emerge refreshed, as though I'd languished in a hot bath.

I wondered about the lives of those nuns, devoid of pleasure and joy. For what sin were they atoning? What were they punishing themselves for? At four in the morning, they'd start praying in a small chapel attached to the convent, kneeling on the cold marble floor. The day ended at nine in the evening, after prayers, and then, every nun retreated to her tiny little cell.

During the day, they worked doing their laundry in the cellar and toiled in the vegetable garden under grim working conditions. Some nuns were relatively luckier and worked in the library, in the office, or as guides.

The work distribution among the nuns was permanent. When she entered the convent, each nun brought a "dowry" of sorts, according to her parents' means. The size of the "dowry" and the novice's education determined her future status and occupation. The poor, low-class nuns were sentenced to the hardest, most demeaning work. The rich ones were given administrative and teaching jobs. The nun's life in the convent wasn't determined by her abilities or personality but rather her lineage and her family's income level.

Even on Sundays, the nuns didn't sleep in. Just like during the weekdays, they got up at four in the morning for prayer, and then went for a walk to a distant hill, about a half-hour walk away. A paved path led to that hill, flanked on both sides by well-tended trees and bushes. On the hill was the statue of Jesus Christ.

We were allowed to accompany the nuns and gladly joined them. We breathed in the fresh air, looked at our surroundings, and felt like prisoners who'd been given a short vacation from prison. The nuns kneeled before the cross, prayed, and turned back. To me, it seemed as though on their way back, they walked jauntily.

I also felt their excitement for the priest's weekly visit. The priest would deliver a sermon at the small church. At the end of the sermon, he alone enjoyed a feast in a room set aside especially for that purpose. The table was set according to French tradition, including glasses for aperitif, water, and wine, and the nuns stood there, prepared to serve him. The priest, who had an impressive paunch, made the most of the hour-long feast. Every time he finished a course, he rang a little silver bell on the table and the nuns hurried in with the next dish.

I watched that absurd scene with mixed feelings. On the one hand, I was pleased to see that there remained a sliver of human emotion in these dried-out husks of women, who came to life in the presence of a man, even if he was a fat, gluttonous priest. On the other hand, what was this foolish fawning for? Was it because since childhood, God was depicted as a man?

Once again, my memory is filled with holes. Who ordered us to leave the convent and move on to Grenoble? How long had we stayed at the convent? It's strange, but the way to the train station is seared in my mind. We walked through the desolate snowy landscape, and two dogs chased us, trying to steal some of the food the nuns gave us for our journey. The dogs were just as starved as we were. They jumped on us and wouldn't leave us until we arrived at the station.

The Catholic Church's approach to the Nazi regime, the occupation, and the persecution of the Jews is a controversial subject. It's well-known that the Holy See in Rome adhered to the Nazi laws, didn't issue enough warnings concerning human rights violations, and didn't voice protests against the annihilation of the Jews. Nevertheless, there is no doubt that there were areas in France in which senior French church officials refused to cooperate with the Vichy regime, which was subservient to the Germans. There were also priests who supported the Résistance, who fought the Germans and helped save the Jews. Among them was Father Glasberg, who dedicated his life to saving Jews.

Glasberg was born to a Jewish family in the Ukraine, and he came to France as a child. I don't know when he was baptized as a Christian, and perhaps his parents converted when he was still a child. He dedicated his life to the priesthood, rose within the Church's hierarchy, and managed to secure a position in the senior office in Lyon. There, he was aware of the suffering of his people. In 1940, he founded The Christian Brotherhood in order to ease the suffering of the multitudes of Jewish refugees who arrived from Germany and lived in terrible conditions. In 1942, when the Germans' grip tightened, The Christian Brotherhood served as a cover for Résistance activity.

The Cardinal of Lyon didn't support the organization's activity and even informed on them, but Father Glasberg was warned beforehand and managed to leave town safely. He spent the years until France was liberated in a small southern town, and it wasn't long before he became an active member of the Résistance.

I found out about his actions many years after the war, and like the pieces of a puzzle, my memories came together and formed a whole picture. Apparently, we were supposed to meet Father Glasberg or one of his people on Lantern Street, but we arrived there a week after he disappeared. The soup kitchen employees, who continued to help those in need, sent us to the convent until we received fake papers.

Even after the war ended, Father Glasberg continued helping

rehabilitate thousands of survivors and assisted the illegal immigration to Palestine and, later on, the immigration of Jews to the State of Israel. He supported the kibbutz movement and was admired by many in Israel, even though he remained loyal to his calling as a man of the cloth in the Catholic Church.

Ruth, 1944.

A GIRL NAMED RENÉE

At the beginning of February 1943, at the height of winter, a girl called Renée Sorel made her way from Grenoble to Moirans. The girl was born in St. Quentin, a town near the Belgian border. Her family moved to Brussels when she was a child, where her father worked as a technician in a textile factory. Her mother died and her father married again. Renée didn't get along with her stepmother. She left home and cut off her ties with her family.

I received papers with the name Renée Sorel from Luciole, a girl active in the Jewish Scouts movement. She also found me work on a farm. Thus, I embraced my new identity so convincingly that I think even a polygraph test wouldn't have revealed the truth.

Lixie found a job as a maid in Grenoble and Frieda as a caretaker in a children's home. We parted ways, and each of us had to cope with her own fate all alone.

I chose my new identity myself. Renée, after the initial of my real name, Ruth. Sorel, because it was easy for me to pronounce and I liked the sound of it. I chose the town of St. Quentin because of its proximity to the Belgian border, which would justify my stiff French accent. I carefully constructed my family story in order to support my circumstances as a girl all by herself.

A bus crowded with passengers brought me to the town of Moirans, where I asked people for directions on how to get to the farm. Farms in France were scattered over great distances. The farmers usually visited town on Sundays to attend church or go to a tavern. The small town contained a school, a post office, and several shops selling basic necessities. Upon coming across an unfamiliar face, the townspeople surrounded me and tried to help me find my way.

"You see the tree over there? Don't go there. The house with the chimney on the left? Don't go there." And more of that.

I walked for an hour on muddy roads until I finally saw a courtyard, which according to descriptions and suggestions, belonged to my farmer. I was tired and hungry, glad to have arrived, when suddenly I discovered an unexpected obstacle—a hidden stream, flowing through the dense vegetation, and over it a bridge made of two logs tied together. I had no choice. I had to cross this rickety bridge while the water flowed rapidly beneath me. At the children's home, it was a well-known fact that if there was a puddle, I would find it. I stood there for a moment, and then, determined and focused, I crossed the bridge without stumbling.

A woman in her late twenties, wearing black and looking much older than her age, met me. "You're Renée? I have been waiting for you since morning. I've soaked the laundry in the bucket. Hurry up. I want you to wash and hang up the laundry before dark."

That was my welcome. No hello, no time to put down my possessions, and no offerings of food. Even animals are led to the trough before they're taken out to work. So, I started working, and with a homemade piece of soap and a scrubbing board, I tried to restore the grayish-black sheets to their original white color. The laundry was filthy. It looked as though it had been used for months without anyone changing it.

At dinner, I sat with the farmer—"the patron"—his wife, and their two-year-old son around a table covered with an oilcloth. We ate potato soup. The farmer, a muscular young man, glanced at me and said, "You have to wash the milk jugs tonight so they'll be ready for the morning milking!" Then he continued eating silently, finished, and went to his room.

I asked the farmer's wife where my room was. She pointed at the stairs that led to the attic, and said, "There's your bed."

"What about sheets and a blanket?" I dared ask.

"Everything's ready there, on the bed."

The floor of the room was made of wood, the ceiling low. A pile of animal feed had spilled in one of the corners. Against the wall, next to the window, stood a bed with a straw mattress covered with a tattered blanket. I lifted the blanket and discovered a filthy, stained sheet, with tangible evidence that a couple had had sex on it frequently. I pulled off the sheet, turned the mattress over, and tried to sleep, but the minute I turned off the light, the room started to rustle with life. Families of rats attacked the animal feed, nibbled, and jumped over me. I left the bed, sat on the windowsill, and waited for dawn. Before my window, a chestnut tree moved its branches, and I imagined it reaching out to console me. I loved that chestnut tree, which was like a friend in this strange and unfriendly place. In the morning, I told the farmer's wife that the rats kept me up all night.

"Ah, I forgot to tell you to take the cat to your room," she said.

The next night, I took the cat, but when the rats emerged, the cat was terrified. It jumped up to the window and scratched the window pane as it yowled desperately. I felt sorry for it and opened the window, and the cat leaped out. Exhaustion overwhelmed me. I got used to the rats, and they got used to me.

It wasn't long before I discovered the farmer was violent. His relationship with his wife was rocky, and his farm was failing. It was a mixed farm, which included crops, a vineyard, a vegetable garden, and geese for fattening. He also had pigs and dairy cows, though none of it was successful. He was cruel to his animals, and they feared him and rebelled against him. When he whipped his horses, they overturned the wagon. When he kicked the cows while milking them, they kicked over the pails and spilled the milk. I witnessed his violent, silent struggle with his animals. I didn't see him beat his wife, but her apathy conveyed a kind of rebellion of the weak. The farmer wasn't a local. He must've bought the farm several years before. He had no social ties with people in the area.

In the summer, every farmer prepared chopped wood for the winter, but not the patron. I had to get up every morning before the family, light the stove, boil water for hot beverages, and cook porridge. How could I light a fire without any wood? I'd collect the pruned branches from among the vines, pile them at the end of the rows, and then drag the piles home. They weren't heavy but tangled, wounding my frozen hands. The pruned branches caught fire easily and produced a bright flame that covered the pots with soot, then quickly extinguished. For a slow and continuous burn, I needed real wood.

So I started collecting the logs around the farm. I split the big ones on a big block in the courtyard. I sawed the thinner branches into pieces for everyday use. Often, the logs weren't adequately dry and didn't catch fire easily. I tried to fan the fire with bellows, as my eyes smarted and filled with tears from the smoke.

I had many responsibilities, and one of them was drawing water from the well in the yard. I'd throw in the torn rope to the bottom of the well. The rough rope wounded my hands.

Everywhere I turned, there was a disaster waiting to happen. The hens laid their eggs in hidden, unexpected places, and every day, the farmer demanded I find all of them. Every day, I cooked leftover cabbage leaves, turnips, and corncobs for the pigs. The pig pen was too small to contain all the fat animals and the fence around it too low. When I approached with the food, they jumped, spilling the food all over themselves and me. And if that wasn't enough, the piglets escaped to the fields through a gap in the fence, with me giving chase breathlessly. Occasionally, the farmer's little boy would also disappear from the yard, and his mother and I would search for him for hours.

When the time came to slaughter the pigs, everything was carefully prepared. The farmers would come and lend a hand, and when slaughtering was over, they celebrated with a lot of food and drink. The pigs were slaughtered in the kitchen, and the screaming was dreadful. The blood was collected in a big pot and cooked with onion, spices, and cream. I would stand in front of the stove, holding a large wooden spoon and mixing the disgusting stew. In the end, they'd fill intestines with the brew, and the result was a "fine sausage." I remembered my mother, who would throw an egg in the garbage in disgust if she saw even a spot of blood. My stomach rebelled and nausea overcame me.

I loved taking care of the rabbits and enjoyed stroking their fur. In preparation for Sunday, the patron would slaughter a rabbit. It was difficult for me to hold the slaughtered rabbit's legs while the patron skinned it. Obviously, I couldn't taste its soft, roasted flesh, which smelled sublime.

The days passed and I formed a routine. Every day, I woke up at dawn and did the same things: searched for firewood, lit the stove, drew water from the well, took care of the pigs, geese, hens, and rabbits, washed the milk jugs, worked in the vegetable garden, and took care of meals and housework. I got used to the farmer's silence, who thought it enough to issue curt orders and had no other interest in me. The food was unvaried. I wasn't always full, but I didn't suffer from starvation. In the evening, I'd fall into my bed, exhausted.

Apart from the farmer and his wife, I didn't meet a living soul except the village madman, who used to come to the kitchen, drunk as a skunk, and follow me around. He'd utter one sentence, which I remember till this day, and he said it with a heavy southern accent while emphasizing the last letter. "I want a wife who knows how to flip an omelet." When he said that, he'd pretend to hold a frying pan in his hand and flip an omelet in the air. After I got to know him, I learned I had nothing to fear from him. I told him I didn't know how to flip an omelet, so I probably wasn't the right woman for him.

After a month, I received my wages and my first day off, so I traveled to Grenoble to meet Lixie, who was my only contact with the world. Lixie was pretty happy. Her employer, Mr. Fortat, was a lecturer at Grenoble University. He was opposed to the German occupation and willingly sheltered a Jewish girl at his home.

I sat in her little room, on a bed covered with pristine sheets. Lixie was wearing a new dress, a present from the family who'd sheltered her. Even though times were hard and products were rationed, this family didn't suffer shortage. Their table was set properly, with beautiful dishes. We went for a walk in Grenoble, a small, clean city, the birthplace of the writer Stendhal. Grenoble was known for the beauty of its surrounding landscape, the snowy mountain peaks, and its green forests in the summer.

I was happy for Lixie's good fortune, but I wasn't jealous. I preferred my circumstances and wouldn't want to be locked up in a little apartment, like she was, under the critical eyes of a bourgeois family, even though all Lixie did all day was dust, set the table, and polish the china and silver. I lived in the open spaces and was well aware that I didn't owe thanks to anyone.

The days grew longer, and there was more work in the fields. We'd go out with long sticks that had a nail attached at the end to weed between the rows of crops. In the early morning hours, we'd collect bugs that threatened to destroy the potato plants from the leaves, and until late at night, we'd stack piles of fragrant hay. The farmer harvested the wheat, and we tied it in sheaves and leaned it one against the other in a round structure to dry until threshing season.

At the beginning of summer, a man arrived at the farm, asking to work. He was wearing rags and looked to be in his fifties. The farmer didn't ask him his name, and called him "Hey you." He didn't even provide him a place to sleep. The man slept in the hayloft, wearing those same sweaty clothes he worked in. He received a plate of food, which he ate somewhere. It was only then that I realized how lucky I was, at least compared to this hired hand, who could be fired any day if the farmer was unhappy with him. I silently objected to this injustice and discrimination, and these experiences probably affected my world view and how I chose to live my life later on.

During that period of work, we all suffered sleep deprivation. The farmer's annoyance grew, and during one of his outbursts, he threw a pitcher of water at me. The next day I told them I meant to leave at the end of the month.

***

In 1942, the British defeated General Rommel's army in North Africa, and at the beginning of 1943, the German Army was defeated in Stalingrad. In July that year, the Allied Forces invaded Sicily and conquered it, and that same month, Mussolini was deposed. News of all these events didn't reach most of the French population, myself included. We only heard about the Germans' victories. I knew that all of Europe was occupied, that a bloody war was taking place in Russia, and that England was bravely resisting the Germans.

France was crawling with Germans, the Gestapo terrorized the people, and those who resisted were tortured in the cellars. Jews were hunted, and those caught were sent to death camps. The young French population was drafted to forced labor in Germany, France was looted of its agricultural products, and the people starved. Vehicles of every kind were confiscated, the roads were empty, and only German cars populated them. Every show of resistance against the Germans resulted in the execution of dozens of hostages.

I knew nothing about my family's situation. My father was in Poland, my mother was in England, Bronia was in Belgium, and Betty, I hoped, was in La Hille. I was all alone, cut off from them, and Lixie was my only contact with the world.

That was the situation when I traveled, one bright summer day, to Grenoble. This time, I had some money I'd earned and a letter of recommendation from the farmer, I was more fluent in French, and I had my new identity as Renée Sorel. I saw an ad from someone searching for a housekeeper, so I knocked on a carved wood door in the prestigious part of town. The proprietress, a slender, thin-lipped woman in her forties, greeted me coolly.

"Renée Sorel?" she asked doubtfully, and examined me from head to toe. The pretentious family name I chose—after Madame Sorel, a lady of the court of Charles VII, King of France, and other famous people in France—didn't correspond with my appearance and class.

The family lived in a three-story house. The floors were covered with expensive carpets, gilt-framed paintings hung on the walls, and the furniture was heavy and old. Apart from the lady, her husband, and their four-year-old daughter, two other young tenants lived in the house, perhaps distant relatives or acquaintances.

It seemed as though the family had seen better days and had once employed many servants, which they now couldn't afford. Nevertheless, they made an effort to maintain some of their old habits. I, for example, was told to wear different aprons and hair covers for every task: a simple blue apron and hat for the laundry and household chores, a light-gray apron and matching cap as a chambermaid, and when I served meals, a tiny white fussy apron and lace cap. I felt ridiculous, as though I were an actress in the theater portraying three different maids.

On my first day, the mistress gave me a tour of the house. We went from one floor to the next, and she gave me various orders. I was surprised to see there was a bathroom on every floor, even though in most houses in France, there wasn't an indoor bathroom. Finally, she showed me my room in the attic. The ceiling of the room slanted, with the higher side about one-and-a-half meters high and the lower side less than one meter. In order to climb on my bed, I had to wriggle in, and sometimes, when I woke up in the morning, I'd bang my head on the ceiling. I asked the mistress which bathroom I could use, and she glanced at me dismissively and said, "On Sundays the public bathhouse is open."

The height of absurdity was during dinner. The table would be set with the best silverware and three types of glasses: A water glass, a wine glass, and an aperitif glass were placed before every person. The mistress weighed, down to the gram, the daily serving of bread. Everyone received their food according to their ration card. Their little girl, who was rationed only 200 grams of bread, received exactly that, after her mother weighed it. Only the head of the family was entitled to talk, and the rest had the right to agree. The master of the house would praise the Vichy regime and criticize the black market and those who needed it.

The meal menu never changed: The first course was a slice of pickled turnip, the main course was lentil stew cooked in water and seasoned with onion, and the third course was fruit, which was abundant this season. After each course, they rang a little silver bell, and I'd arrive, wearing my server's costume, to clear the dishes. At the end of the meal, the wife would scrape all the leftovers onto a serving plate, point at it, and say, "Renée, this is for you."

I would retreat to the kitchen, my throat tight, and between serving them and washing the dishes, I'd try to swallow the food and my humiliation, tears filling my eyes.

During the meal, the little girl would sit in her chair quietly without saying a word. Children weren't allowed to talk during meals, and what was most surprising was that her parents would address her in the third person, as though to emphasize the distance between them.

I remembered how we sat in my parents' house in Berlin, my parents, sisters, and myself, around the *Shabbat* table. We'd talk about everything and laugh at Bronia's baby talk. I felt as though I were suffocating in this large house under the mistress's watchful eye. I feared that before long, she'd suspect my accent and wouldn't hesitate to turn me in. After a month there, my hands were full of sores that refused to heal. I told her I had to take care of the matter urgently and left them.

***

The employment office in Grenoble. I sat on a hard, half-broken wooden bench in a depressing waiting room, among women of all ages who stared with empty eyes at the clerk's door, and waited for my turn. A well-groomed woman in her forties with bleached blonde hair joined the women in the waiting room, looked around, sat next to me, and several minutes later started a conversation. At first, I was suspicious and answered curtly, even though it had been a while since I enjoyed simple human contact. I told her I had several offers of work but I was in urgent need of a reasonably priced furnished room. I mentioned that Grenoble was full of refugees from the north of France, and it was difficult finding accommodations.

"I have connections," the woman said. "I can help you find a clean room at a low price. I also have a dress that no longer fits me and will surely fit you."

I met her that same day at a café, and she brought me a nice flowery summer dress. I quickly took off the brown skirt and striped shirt I'd brought from home, back when I was thirteen, that had been washed one hundred times. When I wore my "new" dress, I felt my feminine confidence return. The woman promised to introduce me the next day to someone who would help me with accommodations.

Indeed, the next day, I saw from afar my new acquaintance, with her bleached blonde hair, walking toward me, accompanied by a huge man whose eyes were sunken in fat. The man wore a white silk shirt and a red tie with a gold pin, and on his sausage-like fingers were gold rings set with precious stones. He studied me lustfully, and when he took my hand, I felt a shudder of revulsion go through my body. I realized I'd been conned, that the blonde had been looking for gullible girls and the disgusting man was the boss. Within seconds, I regrouped, curtsied politely, and with the innocent expression of a good girl told the two of them that I'd reconciled with my parents and I was going back home; therefore, I no longer needed a place to live. I thanked them and left quickly. Nevertheless, something good came out of that meeting—the dress stayed with me.

I found shelter in a place called *Protection de Jeunes Filles* (Protection for Young Girls), which was managed by nuns. Obviously, given my situation, this arrangement suited me much better. The manager was an older nun who registered me, collected a symbolic fee, and explained the rules of the place. "No guests, keep quiet and clean, and be back at the house before eight in the evening."

It wasn't hard to keep to these rules. I had no friends, curfew started at eight, and I was overjoyed to sleep in a bed with clean sheets in the large dormitory, which had two rows of beds along its walls.

The employment office sent me to a workshop that dyed silk kerchiefs. There, in a small room without sufficient ventilation, sat ten women who rolled the edges of the scarves into thin hems and sewed them with a thin silk thread. At the time, these handkerchiefs were in high demand, as they served as a prestigious addition to an old wardrobe. The women who worked there were the wives of laborers whose salary wasn't sufficient to sustain a family.

I was amazed by their openness as they told me about their personal lives, including juicy descriptions of infidelity and love affairs. Another one of their favorite topics was how to get food products. One day, one of the women said that all of the Jews were involved in the black market and knew no shortage, and another woman said, "I hate the Germans but agree with Hitler that the Jews should be destroyed!" They all agreed with her. I kept silent and felt like a coward.

At the *Protection de Jeunes Filles*, things weren't so good either. One day, when I returned from work, one of the girls told me the manager wanted me to go to her office. With a sense of foreboding, I went. She glared at me and said, "Your conduct isn't modest and isn't appropriate for a young girl!"

Apparently, the girls in the room had complained that I undressed and washed myself in their presence. I didn't deny it and explained that when I returned from work sweaty, I washed myself at the sink in the room. I made it clear that I exposed only my upper body, and not, God forbid, all of it. Then I said angrily, "If it's a sin, I plead guilty! What's wrong with maintaining personal hygiene?"

The nun didn't expect such insolence. "You're required to leave within three days," she said curtly.

I assumed my immodesty wasn't the only reason for her decision. I had a feeling I'd aroused her suspicion and she wanted to get rid of the Jew as quickly as possible. And yet, it was the girls who surprised me. Most of them were intimate with random men and proud of it, so what was all the fuss over seeing me bathe?

***

Once again, I searched for a place to stay. At the time, I changed addresses almost every month for various reasons. Once because the rent was too high; once because the room was crawling with disgusting black cockroaches; once because the tenants suspected me. It was hard to find lodgings in the city because its population grew during the war years. Many Jews came to the city, which was under the relatively lenient Italian occupation, and the French Résistance established its headquarters there. Rent was high, I earned a pittance, and I paid a high price for the furnished room I managed to find. The remaining money was barely enough for a few rationed products.

My memory can't be trusted regarding this period. Many details, such as names and addresses, are lost, yet what I do remember clearly, even though fifty years have passed, are the allocated food products I could buy according to my ration card. I belonged to a category of youngsters, so I was entitled to a larger bread ration—350 grams a day. I could exchange that ration for noodles, flour, or other kinds of dough. Every month, I received one kilo of sugar and 300 grams of margarine, according to a calculation of 10 grams per day. Wine was also rationed—a bottle of wine per week. I thought it was generous, but for the French it was a harsh decree. Therefore, they were more than eager to swap wine for bread, eggs, cheese, meat, fish, and potatoes, which weren't included in the rationing during the war. Only toddlers enjoyed a daily ration of milk. The Germans seized all agricultural produce, and the French people were starving. I would buy my ration of bread in the morning and usually ate it right away. I'd boil myself a cup of the brown substance that replaced coffee on a small burner, the only means I had to cook. The only thing I ate was bread with margarine.

During the fruit season, Grenoble was swamped with an abundance of fruit. Cherries, plums, and berries tended to rot quickly, so the Germans didn't bother confiscating them. I ate fruit, like most of the city folks, until I felt I would burst. It was an almost unbelievable sight—the pristine streets of Grenoble were covered with a thick layer of cherry pits, and the townspeople shuffled through them.

However, during other seasons, I existed in a constant state of hunger. The hours that were especially hard were those just before I went to sleep. I'd frequently pass by restaurants with mysterious and alluring names that served pumpkin and turnip stew.

Once, I entered one of those restaurants and ordered a hot stew for several francs and a ration card of ten grams of fat. I sat at a small table, and a young man sat at another table nearby. Suddenly he got up and asked if he could join me because he hated eating alone. I told him that I also preferred company while I ate. We exchanged pleasantries, and he, like a typical Frenchman, complimented me. "I like you. You have all the things I love in a woman."

Not ten minutes had passed and he invited me to spend the weekend with him in the French Riviera. He said he was on his way to his home in Nice to prepare a radio show. We'd eat well and have a nice time, he promised. He was a handsome man, well dressed, with a fashionable haircut, long sideburns, and a small and fair beard, which framed his long, intelligent face nicely. I was silent for a moment, imagining myself with a full stomach after a real feast, sprawling comfortably on a recliner facing the blue sea. Nevertheless, I shook off the daydream, and smiling, I told him that although his offer was charming, my fiancée was returning tomorrow from Lyon and soon I'd be marrying him. The young man stood up, bowed politely, said it was a pleasure meeting me, and left. I'm sure he didn't have any trouble finding another girl to spend the weekend with.

***

I was blessed with robust health and wasn't sick even one day. Even deficient food, the lack of warm clothes, and the torn shoes that water seeped into couldn't bring me down. Only one wisdom tooth that grew crookedly made trouble. One evening I was plagued with an awful, insufferable pain, and in the morning, my face swelled up so badly that I had to go to the dentist. I knew if he treated me, it would relieve the pain, but after paying him, I wouldn't have enough money for my daily bread ration.

I walked the streets helplessly, when suddenly I saw a sign: "Pawn Shop." I realized that was the solution, and I climbed the stairs to the old house's second floor. There, behind the barred window, sat an older man who surveyed me suspiciously. With a pounding heart, I removed the wristwatch my mother had bought me before I left Berlin and pawned it.

I went to the dentist and said, "Pull out the tooth, because I don't have money for other treatments!" I left the tooth at the dentist's and the watch at the pawnbroker's. From then on, during the entire war, I would conduct my life according to the church bells.

***

During the War of Independence, Dadi served in the Oded Division, and from his salary, which he scrimped and saved, he bought me a watch as a gift. A simple, unadorned watch, but nothing could've made me happier.

***

At the time, I looked for a job that would pay me good wages, and in the end, I found one in a workshop for leather wallets.

At the shop's entrance, I was bombarded with the nostalgic smell of leather, which reminded me of Papa and our shop in Berlin. This scent was combined with the powerful smell of glue, which came from a pot standing on a kerosene burner on a long work table.

On both sides of the table, laborers worked, among them a girl apprentice. The radio played incessantly, while the workers sang along with the tunes that were played. We received precut pieces of leather and lining, and after putting together the wallets and purses, we passed them on to be sewn and packed. The work was complicated and required attention to detail and skill. I was an apprentice, the "little hand" of two men who threw long, cheeky glances at me. That was how things were over there; those were the rules of the game. There was no use protesting.

Since I was new, I was sent off on errands, and that's how I first met the workshop's accountant, who sat in a separate room and wasn't seen much. I realized that the accountant was actually the owner of the business, a Jew who had to register his business under the name of one of his French employees. I'm sure he guessed that I was also Jewish and in dire straits. Otherwise, how can I explain the fact that he paid me substantial amounts of money for minor errands?

There is a Chinese proverb that goes like this: "If you have two pennies, buy with the first penny bread to live, and with the second a flower so you'll have something to live for." I didn't buy a flower, but I did sign up for a library membership. For the first time, I had enough money for a deposit, and I resumed my voracious reading. Although they weren't my favorite writers,

I read mainly Balzac and Émile Zola, because that's what I found at the library. I also signed up for night school, for a secretarial course, and learned shorthand and typing. My knowledge, including writing, exceeded that of my classmates, and I found out that the French grammar lessons that I took in Germany were extremely beneficial.

These studies ended unexpectedly. One night, members of the Résistance broke into the classrooms and took all the typewriters. Thus, I lost the money I paid for the course and my chance to receive a certificate.

***

After work, I wasn't in a rush to return to my unpleasant room and wandered along the streets that led to the city's main square. As I walked along aimlessly, I noticed a girl who, just like me, frequently roamed the streets. Her graceful walk and handsome appearance drew my attention. She had long, straight black hair that fell on her forehead, and her glasses emphasized her delicate features. At first, when we passed by each other, we only smiled casually. After some time, we added a slight nod of recognition, and after a while, we said hello. One day we also exchanged several casual sentences, and the cautious overtures continued until we realized the two of us had experienced a similar fate. Charlotte was a Jewish refugee from Berlin who found herself alone in Grenoble.

That same week, Charlotte surprised me when she asked, "Renée, would you like to come with me on Sunday to a meeting of the Zionist Youth Movement?"

"Of course," I answered enthusiastically. "What, those things still exist?"

On Sunday, we took the cable car, which brought us to a ski course, and from there we went to a wood cabin that served as the MJS member's club. The Zionist Youth Movement operated under the cover of a youth association for physical education. I was amazed to find about forty young men and women who sang French songs, then moved on to Hebrew songs, and in the end, sang songs in Yiddish. A young man named Claud belted these out enthusiastically. Toto, the leader of the group, followed the activity of the other youth movements in other cities and updated the group regarding the news of the war from what he heard listening to Radio London.

We strolled along the magical mountainous landscape, played various games, and studied the Bible or Jewish history in small groups. I lived from weekend to weekend, looking forward to the next meeting.

But these meetings had another, unexpected aspect, which emphasized my dire situation. Everyone would bring food for a joint picnic, yet I could only bring bread, which I'd saved all week long. My clothes also weren't appropriate for romping around in the mountains. I'd appear with an old faded skirt that I brought from Germany, while most of the girls wore tight, fashionable trousers. Everyone spoke fluent French peppered with student slang, while I spoke a peculiar mix of high-class French and peasants' dialect. At the end of every meeting, everyone split into small groups to continue their excursions, while I returned alone to my shabby room and read a book, trying to suppress my hunger and my yearning for my family.

Shortly after I arrived at MJS, Leon, one of the members, asked me, "Renée, how do you make a living?"

I was embarrassed. He stood before me, a boy my age, with the ruddy skin of a redhead, and looked at me with a smile that was part shy, part mocking. I realized he'd noticed my desperation, and it was hard for me to pretend.

"I live and work and support myself," I replied with misplaced pride.

"And is your work important to you?" He continued interrogating me.

"It's a job just like any other job. I have to make a living, don't I?"

"Well then, how about joining our group, which is involved in Résistance work? Think carefully before you answer, because this involves risks and an unconventional way of life."

Like the people of Israel at Mt. Sinai, I said, "At your command!"

During my entire period in France, Leon Rottman was like a big brother to me; he guided me, supported me, encouraged me, and demanded of me. He was a modest man, and it was only many years later that I found out about his daring rescue missions.

***

Several days after that conversation, I waited for Thea by the tram station, as agreed. I remembered Thea from those Sunday meetings in the mountains. She was a lively, vivacious young woman and, with her tall stature, dark skin, and black hair, symbolized the image of the pioneer woman in Palestine.

I was tense, wondering what my mission would be. Several minutes later, Thea arrived, and as we pretended to wait for the tram, she explained my mission to me. I hoped to prove that I was daring and sacrificing, but I was told to accompany an old Jew to an old people's home where they'd agreed to hide him. Thea noticed my disappointment and smiled at me, her black eyes twinkling.

"Renée, there are no such things as missions that are more or less important. There are only necessary missions, and even more necessary missions."

I felt as though we understood each other and I'd like working with her.

The man I was supposed to accompany to the retirement home in the nearby town was stubborn, annoying, and slow-witted. I tried to explain to him that, during our journey, we had to pretend not to know each other, he mustn't speak German to me, and he had to pretend he was deaf if someone addressed him. The entire way, things went as planned; the man remained silent and sat at the front of the bus, while I stood in the back. Suddenly the bus stopped, and German soldiers got on and demanded that the passengers step down and present their papers for inspection. The old Jew panicked, ran up to me, and began babbling in German. Fortunately, no one heard him due to the general pandemonium. I grabbed him and said loudly, "What is it, Grandfather, what happened? You can't find your papers? I'll help you." And then I hissed, "For God's sake, be quiet. Everything will be all right."

We arrived safely at our destination, and I learned my first lesson: Even accompanying an old man requires ingenuity and courage.

It wasn't long before I got to know the handful of young men and women in the Grenoble group. I traveled a great deal. Sometimes I took forged documents to someone in another town. These were identity cards, birth certificates, documents stating that their owner had been baptized as a Christian, ration books, and more.

I visited Jews who hid in abandoned buildings in godforsaken places and lived in terrible conditions. I brought them documents and money, as well as news from the outside world, and tried to encourage them to persevere until this nightmare ended, sometime in the future. I mostly traveled by train, never knowing whether I would reach my destination and liaise with the right person. Everything depended on intuition and reacting appropriately at the right moment. No one taught us how Résistance members should behave.

A developed railroad network connected Grenoble with its surroundings, and the French Résistance frequently sabotaged the railroad tracks in order to make it difficult for the Germans to transfer ammunition and soldiers. It so happened that I was frequently stranded somewhere and had to walk to the next station, hoping I'd be able to continue from there.

Once, there was a mishap close to curfew time. I decided to spend the night on the train. I lay down on the bench and fell asleep. In the morning, the train continued after the tracks were repaired, but the car where I slept was disconnected and moved to the side tracks, far away from the station. I woke up and, to my surprise, discovered I was covered with a wool blanket. One of the railroad workers greeted me with a "*Bonjour, ma petite*" (good morning, my little one), poured both of us a warm drink from his thermos, and shared his food with me. It was a small, humane gesture that one cannot forget.

Sabotage of the railway increased. Passengers would take their bicycles with them, and when the train stopped, they would continue this way. But I had a problem—I didn't know how to ride a bicycle, and without one, there was no point in sending me on these missions because the train broke down too frequently.

Now I had two urgent tasks. The first one was to find a bicycle, which wasn't an easy feat at the time; the second was learn to ride one as soon as possible. Fortunately, I found a secondhand bike and did my best to learn how to ride it. When I arrived at the next meeting, proudly riding my new acquisition, my friends received me with a burst of applause.

Grenoble is part of a mountainous region near the French Alps. Riding uphill was hard, while riding downhill was obviously faster and easier. However, speeding downhill almost cost me my life when the front wheel of the bicycle suddenly came loose and I plunged downhill. Fortunately, I managed to turn into a side road, the bike came to a stop against a wall, and I jumped off, unharmed.

Near the river Isère, which crosses Grenoble, was a neighborhood inhabited mainly by large families of Italian immigrants. They had come to France before the war and provided cheap labor. I lived in that neighborhood for a while. My landlady was a plump, kind woman who owned a tavern. Her customers were residents of the neighborhood and Italian soldiers of the occupying army, which ruled the area. The uniform of the Alpine regiments included green felt hats decorated with chicken feathers. The French, who hated the Germans and despised the Italians, thought them ridiculous, but these soldiers walked around with ammunition belts filled with sweets and generously handed them out to the children who gathered around them.

The tiny room I'd rented was on the ground floor, next to the tavern. Sometimes, the landlady would knock on my door at night and bring me a bowl of soup, with the excuse that she had leftovers and it was a pity to waste it. I have no doubt that she guessed I went to sleep hungry. She never asked me what I did or why I was absent so frequently. I'm sure she realized I was involved in matters she was better off not knowing about.

One evening, at the beginning of September 1943, I hurried home, because I was already several minutes late and curfew had begun. The streets were empty, and it was dark. When I arrived home, I found it destroyed. The only thing left was the stairwell, which remained suspended in the air, leading to nowhere. The entire outer wall had collapsed, my bed was buried beneath a thick layer of concrete, and the book *The Red and the Black* by Stendhal, which I'd borrowed from the library the day before, rolled around in the street. I had no other choice. I lay down there, in that place that just that morning had been my room, and made sure no one could see me, because it was forbidden to stay outside during curfew hours. I didn't know what had happened to my landlady.

That night passed slowly, with echoes of explosions, shooting, and screaming from every direction. I waited for morning to come so I'd be able to move and search for a place to spend the next night. When I emerged, I was met by a horrifying sight: Bloody bodies of dead Italians littered the streets, and people hung from the trees of the avenue. It was the first time I had come across such horrifying sights of death. The German troops filled the city, and huge placards screamed from the walls, "The Italians betrayed us and surrendered to the enemy!"

Later, I found out that at the beginning of September, the Allied Forces invaded the south of Italy and brought about its surrender. Things were changing, and it was the beginning of the end of Nazi Germany. Dozens of Jews managed to cross the border to Italy with the Italian soldiers, who retreated in panic.

The Gestapo knew that many Jews found shelter in the area occupied by the Italians and launched a more intensive hunt for them and those resisting the regime. They used a familiar method; they would position themselves around a street or central square and close in on it, and then they would spread all over the area and demand identification papers from all those present. Men who looked Jewish had to drop their pants, and anyone who was circumcised was put on the trucks covered with black canvases.

Several days after the Italians surrendered, I met "Coque," whom I knew from MJS meetings. He was on his way to the post office in Grenoble's main square, and I walked with him part of the way. Suddenly, I noticed something suspicious and only had time to say, "Let's move to a side street and get out of here!"

Just as we started crossing the street, I heard the whistle that signaled the start of the hunt. Soldiers attacked Coque and pulled his pants down. From the corner of my eye, I saw them kick him and shove him onto the truck. I continued walking without disclosing that we knew each other.

I told the other members that Coque had been taken. I didn't know his real name and didn't know the circumstances that brought him to Grenoble. He was taken on his last journey, but perhaps he managed to escape and survive. Perhaps he's still alive somewhere in the world. I will never forget his face as he stared from the truck to the street, the utter despair in his eyes. I will also never forget my shame for abandoning him to his fate. But at the time, those were the rules of the game.

We held an emergency meeting as a result of the new situation and decided that the men would move to the German opposition centers, which were in the vicinity of Toulouse. The organization *Armée Juive,* the Jewish Army, set up in advance hiding places. There, the members participated in weapons practice and left to take part in sabotage and Résistance missions, coordinated with the French Maquis Résistance movement. The girls stayed in Grenoble with George, another member of the movement, and Toto and continued with their activities.

I moved into the room of one of the boys who left town and joined the Maquis. My landlords were two elderly people who lived with their son on the fifth floor of a large building, while my room, in the attic, was originally intended for storage and not habitation. The water faucet was located one story below, and the outhouse was in the yard, as was customary in France. The landlords' fool of a son was neglected and smelly and at night loitered by my room, making animal sounds. I was afraid of him and would invite homeless girls and boys to sleep in my room. That way, I could help others and also feel safe from that madman. But the neighbors noticed men and women climbing to the fifth floor and spending the night there, and after complaining to the police's department of ethical standards, an investigation was launched. Fortunately, I found out about it ahead of time, as the elderly landlords told me. I paid my rent plus a hefty additional sum and left at once.

Our group had grown significantly smaller. Most of the young men moved to the Résistance organizations in the mountains, and the remaining girls worked hard to carry out the assignments. We worked diligently to manufacture fake documents and provided the merchandise all the way to Lyon and Nice. We found a new method to ensure the documents would pass all the inspections and checks. We traveled to villages, met with the village mayors, and tried to convince them to "resuscitate" young men and women who'd passed away and delete the clause declaring their death. We submitted these documents, with the pictures of whoever had them, to the Ministry of the Interior for registration and confirmation.

It wasn't easy convincing those mayors. At first, the girls applied reasonable moral pressure while hinting that when the day of liberation arrived, they'd be happy to testify that the mayor cooperated with the enemy. Sometimes they also threatened that the Maquis would know how to take care of them. I was never among the girls who used those methods to convince others, nor did I have the agility of Therese, our Parisian, who knew how to turn the clerks' heads in the offices and leave with stamps or documents that she stole out of the pockets of their coats that hung in the corridors.

Leaving a good impression, radiating innocence and trustworthiness—those were my advantages. I was the one who submitted—taking on the role of the secretary of a make-believe town—a document with a passport picture to the Ministry of the Interior. I would sit before the clerk, who carefully checked the documents and pictures, and pray that these pictures of young people with Jewish features wouldn't give me away. I would enter the office with a shy, innocent smile, while in my heart, I wondered whether I'd leave smiling or whether my deception would be exposed. George and Thea would anxiously wait for me outside, and when I'd leave the lion's den, holding a stack of approved documents, they'd heave a sigh of relief. Had I been arrested, they'd have had no way to help me. Nevertheless, knowing that my friends were waiting for me outside strengthened my spirit, encouraged me, and instilled in me confidence that everything would be all right.

At the same time, we'd accumulate the ration books of Jews who'd managed to cross the border to Switzerland or Spain. My job was to present those books and receive for them a monthly supply of ration stamps. I would make up various excuses as to why the owners of these books never showed up and learned to lie without a qualm.

During the years 1943–1944, our main effort was focused on smuggling children to Switzerland. We smuggled only children, because the Swiss government sent back all the adults who managed to reach the border. From there, they were captured by German patrols. Gathering the children and smuggling them over the border was a difficult operation. First, we located families with youngsters of the appropriate age and convinced them to give us their children. I went from family to family in remote villages. I realized that in order to gain the parents' trust, I had to speak their language. I spoke broken Yiddish, which was actually broken German. I mentioned my own mother, who was forced to send off her children in 1939 to save them. If there was someone who could feel their pain of separation, it was me. I knew that separation may be permanent.

Smuggling a large group was a complicated operation because of the poor transportation conditions and absence of means of communication. One time, I was supposed to smuggle twenty-five children. When the day arrived, the group came to the Grenoble train station and from there was supposed to board the train to Annecy. When they arrived, I surveyed their features and thought, *God, why do they look so Jewish? If it were only one of them, but the entire group?* To me, it seemed as though their Jewishness was glaring.

We arrived at Annecy, and I brought the children to the

collection point in the gym of a school. We gained permission to use the auditorium thanks to my "good impression show." I presented myself as someone who was organizing a group of children to go on vacation in Switzerland and needed a rest stop for them. We were indeed sending children, but Jewish children, not French, and in order to cross over the Swiss border. It was something entirely different.

A team of three—Bella, Ado, and myself—had to look after the children's needs. We played with them in order to calm them, we passed the time, and we tried to help them forget their fear. In the end, we had to stay in Annecy for one more day because something went wrong with our original plan. We decided the children had to eat one warm meal. In order to reach the restaurant, we had no choice but to pass by the Gestapo building. We passed by in threes, loudly singing French folk songs. Despite my fear, I felt an almost childish satisfaction that we dared pass so cunningly under the Germans' noses.

It was zero hour. Mariana, who was in charge of passing the children to the border smuggler, accompanied them to the border town of Annemasse, and from there, for a substantial sum of money, the "guide" was supposed to smuggle them at night through German lines. Bella, Ado, and I stayed in the empty gymnasium and waited for morning. The hours passed slowly. None of us managed to sleep, and that night, I lit my first cigarette. When we heard that the children passed safely, we were terribly relieved. We scattered quickly and rushed to relay the good news to the frantic parents.

The guide also brought the money we needed. The money, the

number-one means for our operations, was sent by the American Joint Distribution Committee. Our liaison and address in Switzerland was Heini Bornstein, who later became a member of Kibbutz Lehavot HaBashan.

In La Hille, the only children left were those younger than fifteen, under the protection of the Swiss Red Cross, among them my sister Betty. I started trying to bring her to Switzerland. I sent a letter to Eugen Lyrer. I knew he'd be willing to help. I wrote to him that his "family," meaning Switzerland, was inviting Betty to stay with them. We set a day and hour to bring Betty to his relatives. On the set day, I waited for Lyrer at a café in Annecy.

I wasn't sure he even understood what I meant, and if he did, whether he'd risk himself and come to our meeting. Of course, I also didn't know if he'd manage to arrive at the set date. But he did and Betty was with him. He hadn't let me down.

Betty, whom I hadn't seen for an entire year, was now almost thirteen. She hadn't changed and was still that thin, pale girl who looked younger than her age. We hugged, my eyes full of unashamed tears, and it was only then that I realized how much I'd missed her. Eugen Lyrer left us and hurried back to La Hille. Perhaps he was punished for acting against the accepted rules of an employee of a Swiss institute. Later, I remembered I'd forgotten to reimburse him for his travel expenses, which he must've paid from his modest salary.

The weather was fine, so Betty and I walked through the beautiful town on the shores of placid Lake Annecy. The mountains around were snowy. On the bank facing the lovely promenade, we saw houses with red roofs surrounded by greenery.

The bridge railing was made by an artisan blacksmith. The few picturesque streets were covered by arches, and the shop windows were tastefully decorated yet didn't contain much merchandise. It was the same town in which I'd wandered one year ago with Lixie, hungry and desperate, searching for a place to lay my head for the night. This time Annecy welcomed me, and I viewed it as a sort of personal victory over my hardships.

I tried to spoil Betty, as much as was possible at the time. I bought her ice cream made from sweet water and cookies made from bran and artificial sweetener. When evening came and it was time for us to say goodbye, Betty clung to me and begged to stay with me. I became tough again and said, "There's no way you can stay with me. Get on the train!"

Betty arrived safely in Switzerland, but her years there were hard and miserable. At first, she stayed at a refugee camp for several months. Then she lived with a family in Schaffhausen, a town that was bombed. She was fourteen when she was sent to work for a terminally ill woman. She took care of her day and night without receiving any compensation. At the time, my thin little Betty suffered from weakness and a constant low fever that weren't treated. Years later, when she underwent tests to find out why she couldn't conceive, she found out that during her time in Switzerland, she'd contracted tuberculosis. She remained childless.

***

Not always did smuggling children to Switzerland pass smoothly. One of the victims was Mariana. She didn't stand out in her appearance. She was just a regular girl, her brown hair combed to the side, her face round and open. I heard she was an excellent student and was especially good at math, and that impressed me greatly. She arrived in Paris as a child. Her father, so I was told, was a high court judge in Germany and left when the Nazis came to power. She spoke fluent French with a strong Parisian accent. I knew her from the MJS meetings, but I don't remember us ever talking. She lived in Lyon and took part in the group's operation of smuggling children to Switzerland. She'd take the children who arrived at Annecy to Annemasse and hand them over to the border smuggler. She did that many times, and rules of caution dictated that it was time to replace her. I offered myself instead, but Mariana refused and said that it would be a shame to waste her experience.

We considered the pros and cons and decided she'd go on one last operation. And it was indeed her last time. Mariana was captured near the border, brought to the Gestapo, and tortured. They wanted her to disclose the names of her friends. She remained silent, didn't disclose the names, and was executed.

After the liberation, we went to search for the place where she was murdered. Locals led us to a grove outside the city, and there we found her body with the bodies of other prisoners who'd been shot. Today in Yad Vashem, there's a little garden in Mariana Cohen's memory, next to the auditorium dedicated to French Jewry.

***

Mariana's death was constantly on my mind. Once again, fate had spared me. Had my request to replace Mariana been accepted, perhaps I would've paid with my life and she would've survived. After that, I was filled with confidence that I'd emerge unscathed from every situation, that I'd live to see the end of the war and immigrate to Palestine. Another thought plagued me: Would I be able to endure torture without revealing my friends? I was much more afraid of revealing names than I was of death. I'm sure that every person who's ever been involved with Résistance activity was familiar with this fear.

***

At the beginning of 1944, we were joined by a girl who was my age. Her name was Raymonde. She was tall, broad-shouldered, and friendly. We didn't ask unnecessary questions, we didn't know each other's real names, and we didn't tell each other about ourselves and our families. We managed to rent a room and a half on the second floor of a building together, and for the first time since I left my family, I lived in a nice furnished apartment, with a kitchenette, a burner, and a toilet. So much light filtered through the windows, and we could watch the red roofs of a convent that had a yard full of chestnut and plane trees. Further down the street was a big building that housed the city's Gestapo headquarters. Sure of myself, I'd fearlessly strut by the guards with my head held high. In our apartment building, there were six apartments, two on every story, and I rarely met the other tenants in the stairwell.

Gas for cooking was supplied only two hours a day, and we used it to cook any vegetable we could get. Sometimes at noon, our friend Shuka came to visit, bringing with him potatoes, beans, and onions, which were rare and precious products. The three of us would sit around the table and enjoy the tasty, filling soup.

Shuka, which was what everyone called him since the time he was in the Scouts Movement, was a bit older than us and had starting studying law in Paris. He paid for his tuition by tutoring a fourteen-year-old girl from a rich Jewish family, and the two of them fell in love. With her parents' permission, they got engaged. Their only condition was that he wait until she reached the age of nineteen before they got married. His beloved's parents, who hid in one of the villages in the area, provided him with all the food he brought us. It wasn't long before someone else joined our table—Paul, whom Shuka knew from Paris. Our apartment became a home to him too. Paul was seventeen, a gorgeous blond, and he seemed to me like a person who needed taking care of.

We were in constant danger of being caught and sent to our deaths. So, with this awful threat hovering over our heads, Shuka's story seemed like a magical fairy tale; a level-headed young man, both reserved and rational, found the love of his life, a child really, ten years younger than him. Shuka's belief that those years of horror would pass, that he'd live with his beloved, gave us hope. Indeed, Shuka and his intended bride survived those difficult years, returned to Paris, and got married.

***

At the beginning of 1944, the hunt for Jews and members of the Résistance was at its peak. Under those circumstances, our meetings in the mountain cabin came to a stop. Sometimes, on Sundays, we met at Madame Jeanne's home, on the outskirts of town. Several of us girls would meet there and enjoy each other's company. I'll write later about the glorious Madame Jeanne and her activities.

Although each of us lived and operated separately, we sometimes craved each other's company. We gratefully accepted an invitation from Bobby, a seventeen-year-old boy from the MJS, to visit a village near Grenoble, where his mother, a doctor, was staying with his little brother.

It was a cold and gloomy morning when eight of us girls met at her house. This gathering was explicitly against Toto's instructions and rules. But Bobby's mother turned out to be such a welcoming woman. We enjoyed her warmth and the homey feeling in her attic apartment. We browsed the many books she managed to bring with her from Paris, looked at photos from better days, and played with Bobby's little brother. When the sun peeked out from among the heavy clouds, we went outside and took a group photo to immortalize the moment, a day so different from the succession of gray days.

Shortly after our visit, Bobby's mother and little brother were caught. Bobby was the only one who managed to escape. I was consumed with guilt because I was sure our group's visit was what caused their arrest. Only later did I find out that Bobby's mother was a member of the French Résistance and someone denounced her. She and her little son perished. Bobby immigrated to Israel and lives in Jerusalem.

In addition to our daily fear that the Germans would capture us, we also suffered from food shortage. I no longer received my daily ration of bread, and bread had no replacement. All that was left of my shoes was the upper part, and when the snow melted, I waded through murky, cold snow, with no chance whatsoever of obtaining another pair of shoes. I'd brought my winter coat made from quality wool from Berlin, but it fit a thirteen-year-old girl. I sold the coat and bought instead a thin coat with no lining. Although it was my size, it didn't protect me from the winter gales of the Alps.

***

Paul Roitman, who is now a rabbi in Jerusalem, suggested we renew our Bible lessons and that they take place in our apartment. Before long, we had a small group of girls who studied the Bible enthusiastically. I doubt if these lessons added anything to my knowledge of Hebrew, but I have no doubt that they cheered me up. I felt as though we had the power to overcome our daily hardships and maybe the day would come and we would be able to immigrate to Israel. There was a purpose to our struggle and a goal to our lives.

One ordinary morning, Raymonde woke up early and left the house with a stack of forged documents. I woke up late and prepared to leave when I heard pounding on the door. I looked through the peephole and saw three German soldiers.

The rifle butts banging against the door and the yelling of "Open up!" sent me five years back, to the day the Gestapo pulled my father out of his bed just before dawn. My heart skipped a beat. I plastered a fake smile on my face and, with shaking hands, opened the door. One soldier stood before me, his rifle aimed at me, while the other two burst inside and, within a minute, emptied everything in the closet and drawers and threw them on the floor.

A million thoughts ran through my head. Why were they searching our apartment? Would they search all the other apartments in the building? Had they come to the wrong address? Good thing Raymonde had already left with the forged documents. The soldiers didn't find anything suspicious, but suddenly I remembered the Bible Paul Roitman had left behind, which we hid beneath the mattress. *Maybe tossing and upturning drawers was enough and they wouldn't search the area of the bed*, I hoped as I pressed against the wall. Suddenly my knees started shaking of their own volition. I couldn't control them. God, I prayed, please don't let them search the bed. My prayers fell on deaf ears. With one rough movement, the soldiers turned the mattress, and their officer picked up the book, shook it, saw the strange letters, and turned to me.

"What's this?"

"Oh, this is a book in Arabic that I got from my fiancé who lived in Algiers before the war and volunteered to work in Germany."

"And why is this book under the mattress?"

"My fiancé told me to put it beneath the mattress. It would

keep me and our love safe," I answered with a coy smile. I guess the young soldiers liked my story, because they thought the French were proficient in matters of love. The three knocked their heels, saluted "Heil Hitler, Mademoiselle," and left.

I remained standing against the wall for some time, my knees still shaking, thoughts running through my mind. Whose suspicions had we aroused that they informed on us to the authorities? They probably hadn't thought we were Jews, but members of the French Résistance.

I waited for Raymonde to return, and when she did, we packed our few belongings and quickly and sorrowfully left our lovely apartment before it became a trap. We couldn't afford to be picky and rented the first free room we found, in a cheap hotel. Dubious faces stared at us in the hallway. The hotel was populated with criminals, whores, and their pimps, as well as guests who were relatively more respectable. The worst waited for us at night: swarms of fat, huge cockroaches, with shiny armor, the likes of which I'd never seen before. Those cockroaches were that disgusting hotel's real owners. I pulled the blanket over my head and fell asleep.

***

During all those difficult months, I kept in touch with Lixie, who since her arrival at Grenoble worked as a maid for the Fortrat family. Lixie had been a lively girl, and both girls and boys craved her company, but her position as a maid was slowly sucking the life out of her. The dull routine of a housemaid, her helpless feeling of dependence, the lack of challenges and stimulation, dulled the sparkle in her eyes. I went to visit her, and Madame Fortrat welcomed me kindly. She knew I was Jewish, like Lixie, and she liked my Zionist opinions and the idea that one day the Jews would return to the land of Israel. I felt that her enthusiastic support of Zionism stemmed from her desire to get rid, elegantly of course, of French Jewry.

When I saw Lixie's despair, I suggested to her that she leave her position and join our group. I told her, "There's a lot of work and you fit. You're blonde, your facial features aren't Jewish, you speak good French, and you're quick and resourceful. You belong with us."

We sat in her little room, on her bed with the pristine sheets, a tray before us with delicate china saucers containing warm tea. Lixie shook her head. "No, Ruth, I can't live like you do. I need my own clean and protective corner. I don't have the courage to give up a comfortable life and move from place to place, live in filthy rooms without basic comforts and without knowing what the day will bring."

As I listened to her, I recalled Lafontaine's fable about the city mouse who lived a good life between the walls of a house, and the country mouse who had to scramble to survive but was free and independent. The truth was that there was another reason Lixie refused to leave the Fortrat family—there was a budding love affair between her and the Fortrats' son. Pierre was Lixie's age. He was tall, with a long neck and small head, and his face was handsome. A baby face. His parents sensed that something was happening between them, and things had become tense.

I reminded Lixie of all the romances we'd read, about the passionate love affairs between the master's son and the sweet little chambermaid. The noble boy would promise, vow really, to stand by his beloved's side in thick or thin, even if his family would disown him. The maid would be tempted and end up being sent away in shame.

I told Lixie, "Who's your Pierre? A little boy, tied to his father's table and his mother's apron strings. Without them, he's lost. Of course he'll bow to his parents' wishes."

One day, Madame Fortrat received two theater tickets to a play by the famous Catholic playwright Paul Claudel. She gave Lixie the tickets, and Lixie invited me. I forgot the plot of that play, but for some strange reason, its name is seared in my mind: *The Tidings Brought to Mary*. The play was glaringly Christian, and when we left the theater, Lixie told me casually, "You know, Ruth, I believe in that."

I was furious and said, "Nonsense! Don't tell me you believe Maria gave birth and remained a virgin, and that Jesus was God's son, who was resurrected. You want to believe because of your love for Pierre, but even if you convert and become a believing Catholic, it won't change anything. The Fortrat family will never accept you."

Lixie wasn't the only one who considered running away from her Judaism.

I met Frieda by chance during one of my many journeys. She worked under a false identity as a caretaker in one of the many children's homes in the French Alps. After exchanging several sentences, she said to me, "I'll have you know that I'm

French now, and I'll remain French. From today, I'll no longer be a Jew!"

My answer was, "Well then, I wish you all the best. But here is where we say goodbye."

But life holds many surprises. Ten years later, I found a postcard in my mailbox. It was written in French, signed by Frieda. This was what she wrote:

Hello, Ruth.

I found out you live in Kibbutz Lehavot HaBashan. I live in Netanya and would love to meet you.

Will you forgive me? If so, I'll come to visit you.

I was shocked. Frieda had immigrated to Israel and lived in Netanya. Both of us were grown women, married with children.

And yet, she still feared I held a grudge because of things that had been said when our circumstances had been so different. Was I so uncompromising that the things I said held such weight?

***

Lotte grew up in Germany, in a traditional Jewish home. She was with us in the children's home and managed to escape to Switzerland at the end of 1942, where she was taken in by a priest. After that, she converted to Christianity. After training to become a social worker, she worked as a missionary for many years in Korea and Angola. At the age of fifty, she decided to immigrate to Israel, studied Hebrew, and for ten years, taught the blind. She returned to her people, but not to her faith.

Werner, whose story I told in the previous chapters, also hid his Jewish roots and lived his life in the United States, fully denying his origins. It was only well into his seventies that he told his children his secret.

Perhaps there are more people among the La Hille group that denied their Jewish origins, for a while or forever, following those terrible years of persecution and the threat of annihilation.

***

In the height of winter, I was sent to the hill town of Briançon near the Italian border. This time my mission was a bit different. I wasn't sent to visit Jews in hiding, but to meet a man named Ricardo Lopus and receive a message from him. As was customary, I didn't ask questions.

Briançon was high in the Alps, in what was for me an unfamiliar area.

When I arrived at my destined train station, I found out that the town was several kilometers from the station and very high up. I had no choice but to start climbing the steep path by foot.

After some time, I arrived at the town's sole main road. From the houses and stores, I perceived that in peacetime the locals made their living from wealthy tourists. On the ridge, which was much higher than the street, I saw many convalescence homes, which I found out were for tuberculosis patients. I could make out the patients lying on recliners on the balconies, covered with wool blankets. They lay in the cold and hoped that the fresh mountain air and sun would help them, just as was written in *The Magic Mountain* by Thomas Mann. At the time, tuberculosis was a common, threatening disease that killed many people and there wasn't a cure for it.

I was tired from the climb and from searching for the address and struggling with the thin mountain air. I stood before a convalescence home where I was supposed to meet Ricardo. It was approaching noon, and I knocked on the front door. The woman who opened the door asked me what I wanted, and I asked her to tell Ricardo that Renée wished to see him. "Wait here, I'll call him," the woman said.

I stood in the large, dim foyer. Who was this man and what was the purpose of my mission? Several minutes passed, and a tall, handsome man who looked to be about twenty appeared and shook my hand. "Matron told me a Spanish girl was here to visit me," he said with a smile.

He tilted his head toward me, and soft brown eyes looked at me and caressed me. Love at first sight, we say in English, but the French expression, "*le coup de foudre*" (struck by a thunderbolt), is more accurate for what I felt just then. I stood there, as though frozen in place, my entire being electrified by Ricardo's presence.

"Let's get out of here so we'll be able to talk more freely," he said, gently touching my elbow and leading me through the corridor outside. That light touch made me tremble.

We walked down the path to the main road. Ricardo said that it would be another two days before he'd be able to contact another liaison, from whom he'd receive the necessary information. I found out that Ricardo, as one of the lodgers in the sanatorium for tuberculosis patients, didn't arouse any suspicion; therefore, he was an important link for Maquis in the area and a useful liaison. I realized I was sent to coordinate a joint operation between Maquis and the AJ, which was the Jewish Army organization. Most of the MJS members were also members of the AJ but kept it a secret. The AJ was involved in armed conflict, acts of sabotage, and the execution of informants and collaborators.

I agreed with Ricardo that we'd meet in the afternoon and went to search for a room for several days, while he returned to the convalescence home for the siesta.

In normal times, Briançon, a holiday resort, would have been full of tourists, but due to the war, there were few, and I easily found accommodation. I sprawled on the bed and tried to rest a bit, but to no avail. I left the room and went to meet Ricardo long before our set time. From a distance, I noticed he was already waiting for me. "My heart told me you'd be early," he said.

We laughed, loudly and unselfconsciously, as though we'd known each other for a long time. And Ricardo, as though it was the most natural thing in the world, put his arms around me.

Thus began four beautiful days. Ricardo told me about his family in Barcelona. He told me how much he missed Spain and about his passion for music. He came from a large, respectable Spanish family, and many of its sons were well-known musicians. He was supposed to study in the conservatory, but when the civil war broke out, he joined the socialists who fought Franco. His hope was to see the end of Franco's dictatorship and return to his country.

Suddenly, I was telling him about me, talking about myself, my parents, the loneliness that was my constant companion ever since I lost my family. These were things I'd never told anyone until now, including my yearning for Israel and my desire to become a pioneer and live in a society that believed in equality and social justice. We made the most of every hour of the day. He broke the rules of the convalescence home, while I discarded all warnings regarding his frightening, contagious disease. Nothing else mattered but the two of us and the magical view around us. We walked for hours along the breathtaking edge of the canyon. On the cliff before us, we saw the entrances to caves with long icicles hanging over the abyss. The sun touched them and they sparkled like diamonds. Was it real? A world as such existed only in fairy tales.

At the end of the week, the other man appeared and Ricardo gave me the information. During our last evening together, we sat at a café in Briançon wrapped up in each other, uncaring of our surroundings. We barely touched our food. Ricardo, as he tended to do, leaned toward me, took my hands in his, and the look in his eyes filled me with love. Suddenly I tensed. I heard a group speaking German. A group of German soldiers on leave sat at a nearby table and studied us.

"Look at those two lovers!" I heard them say. "These French. There's no one like them in matters of love."

I couldn't contain my laughter and told Ricardo, "Look at us.

We're sitting right beneath their noses, a young man fighting for socialism and a Jewish girl whose blood is cheap. Isn't this our victory over evil?"

The next day, it was time to say goodbye. Ricardo walked me to the train station down below. I wanted to protest but didn't dare. How would he climb the steep incline back up to the town? He was so weak from his illness. The train started moving, and through eyes blurred with tears, I saw Ricardo run after the train, waving frantically.

I returned to Grenoble and kept the memories of those wonderful days to myself. It was pointless telling the others what had happened to me in Briançon, and besides, I also lacked the words to express those powerful feelings I'd experienced. I wrote several letters to Ricardo without stating my address in order not to endanger our network.

At the end of the war, when I was already a kibbutz member in Israel, I renewed my correspondence with Ricardo. He was still in the sanatorium. He wrote to me that he admired me for realizing the ideals of socialism. After some time, I received a letter with a different address, in which he wrote that he was leaving the sanatorium and getting married soon. I hurriedly wrote back and congratulated him. But I didn't receive an answer. Several weeks passed and I found my letter to him in my mailbox. On the envelope, it was written, "Undeliverable. Recipient deceased." Had his illness returned and finally overwhelmed him? Or had he met some other disaster? I would never know.

***

A slow train made its way from Lyon to St. Etienne and from there south, to the towns and villages of the area. Once every so often, it stopped at sleepy stations that looked alike; the only difference was the changing signs. At every station, the villagers boarded and got off the train, and it seemed as though they all knew each other. The passengers exchanged greetings, talked about the weather and the state of the fields, and passed among themselves a round straw basket holding a bottle of wine. They were used to drinking without touching the lip of the bottle; only their bobbing Adam apples indicated they were taking crude gulps.

They stared at me suspiciously, and I started to feel uncomfortable, a stranger among locals. When the train reached my destination, I was the only passenger who got off. The station guard returned immediately to his office, and the platform was empty of people. My uncomfortable feeling increased. How would I find the man to whom I had to give the large amount of money I had on me as well as the documents?

While I considered whether to disturb the guard's rest or make my way to the town, I heard shouting behind me. "Hey! You there, don't move!"

Two militia men wearing black uniforms pointed their guns at me and crossed the railroad tracks. God, had I fallen into a trap? I realized I had to keep my cool and not show fear, so I walked toward them, my head held high. They brought me to a nearby hut, me leading and the two of them behind me. Once in the hut, the older man dropped into an armchair behind a desk and set his rifle aside. The younger one, who stood next to me, also set his rifle aside but pointed a gun at me.

"What's your name?" the older one interrogated me. I gave him my legitimate identification papers from Grenoble.

"Nevertheless, Mademoiselle Renée Blanc"—I'd changed my name—"what brings you here?" he asked with a mocking smile on his face. My mind worked overtime. We were amateurs and we relied on our luck. I hadn't received any instructions regarding how to behave in such a situation. What would be my excuse for the large amount of money in my purse? I'd hidden the documents in my underwear and knew that if they searched me, they'd find them.

"I'm the housekeeper of a respectable man, a professor at the University of Grenoble. He's ill and sent me to find a place where he can convalesce."

That was it. That was the reason I was in the area, and it also explained the money in my pocket.

"What's the name of your professor, Mademoiselle Blanc?" the officer asked.

"Monsieur Fortrat," I heard myself say, and was seized with fear. How could I have done that? How had that happened? Why had I disclosed the name of the Fortrat family and endangered them and Lixie? But it was too late now. When I was asked to provide an address, I gave them a fake one.

The militia man wrote something in his diary, got up, and left the hut. It was noon and he must've gone to eat. Now the young man sprawled in the armchair, still aiming his gun at me. *Now is the time*, I thought to myself, and I shyly asked to go to the bathroom. He got up and escorted me to a temporary structure built on a hole in the yard, all the while holding his gun. Inside the outhouse, I got rid of all the documents, and with a heavy heart, a considerable amount of money. I tore the documents into tiny pieces and threw them into the hole. I left the outhouse with a sense of relief and a smile. The young man stood where I left him, still aiming his gun at the door.

The hours crawled by, the men took breaks to eat and rest, and I still stood against the wall, without eating or drinking anything since early in the morning. In the evening, the officer in charge arrived, wearing a fancy black uniform, rows of military decorations on his chest. He studied the papers before him for a long time, then raised his head, stared at me lengthily, and suddenly said, "You're a Jew!"

I tensed. The thirst and hunger and aching feet suddenly seemed so inconsequential. I stood with my legs planted firmly, my hands shoved in my pockets, looked him in the eye, and said,

"No, Sir, I'm not a Jew. What is a Jew?"

But he insisted. "You're a Jew! I know you are!"

I answered brazenly, "You want to force me to lie. Fine. As you wish. I'm a Jew."

My impudence worked. He indifferently repeated several questions, studied my documents again, and emptied my bag. After some time, he leaned back in his armchair, looked at the window, and casually said, "The train to Grenoble is leaving in several minutes. Get out of here and don't you dare show your face here again!"

I'll never know why they didn't arrest me, what they suspected, and why they released me so suddenly. When I arrived at Grenoble, it was dark. The curfew had begun, and I used side streets so I wouldn't come across German patrols. When I opened the door, Raymonde hugged me frantically and started crying. "I was sure you were caught and I would never see you again!" she said.

"I was very close to that," I said, and told her everything.

I never told anyone that I slipped and almost brought disaster to a devoted family and my friend Lixie.

***

Forty years later, I met Lixie, who came from the United States to a gathering of the La Hille children that took place in Kibbutz Lehavot HaBashan. When we talked about the "old days," I told her about my slip of the tongue that long-ago day. She was horrified and reacted badly. "How could you have endangered us like that?"

It was as though forty years hadn't passed and the danger still existed. In the letters that she later sent me from the United States, she continued expressing her fear and imagining the consequences that my slip of tongue could've caused. And truly, how could I have explained my behavior? But it had happened.

***

It was almost 11 a.m. when I climbed five floors and knocked on the attic door of the apartment on Saint Peres Street. Sabin opened the door and said, "Renée, everyone's waiting for you."

I was late because I had difficulty finding the place. It was the first time I entered the "Holy of the Holies," the lab, the center where documents were forged. I stared at all the machines in wonder.

Just an hour before, I stood with Thea by the tram stop, where we'd met as though by chance and planned the day's activities. From afar, I saw Madeleine walking toward us quickly. Madeleine worked for the OSE, an organization founded by French Jewry before the war, which helped children of Polish immigrants and Jewish refugees from Nazi Germany. Madeleine worked with the organization in Paris, and after the occupation of Paris, she moved south to Free France, where she continued her work. Until the middle of 1942, the organization operated officially, and then semi-officially, while cooperating with Résistance groups.

I only knew Madeleine by sight. She was older than us, reserved, withdrawn, and cool. This time, from afar and as opposed to her usual manner, she waved at us excitedly.

"Oh, good thing I met you!" she said. Then she told us that several weeks ago, a baby had been brought to an orphanage. The baby's parents, two young German Jews, were in hiding and lived in miserable conditions. The Gestapo had found them and they were arrested. In the mother's purse, they found the address where the baby was staying. That morning, the matron of the orphanage received notice that the Gestapo would arrive the next day at approximately 4 p.m. to take the baby, and she had to be ready to give her over. The matron came to Madeleine to consult with her. Madeleine tried to convince her to give her the baby, but to no avail. The manager refused. She was terrified of the Germans. "Do something! Save Corinne!" Madeleine begged tearfully. She gave us the address of the orphanage and the name of the baby and left.

Thea and I stood, bemused and silent. We were just put in charge of the fate of a helpless creature.

"The matron will give the child only to the Germans!" I said. "Unless I'm the German who'll receive Corinne!"

Thea asked, "Are you telling me that you'll go there instead of the Gestapo?"

"Yes. Do you have a better suggestion?"

In the lab sat George, Leon, Sabin, Thea, and myself. We deliberated whether we should undertake such an operation. Was saving the life of a baby worth the risk? I sat silently, not participating in the argument, until I suddenly burst out, "We know the Germans are making selections, deciding who will live and who will die. They only let those who are useful to them live. Are we going to be like them? We have only one way. If there's a chance to save someone, we have to act, immediately and without over thinking it!"

So, it was decided. We decided to act as quickly as possible.

At a quarter to three, I was ready, wearing a long, ungainly raincoat, similar to those the Gestapo women wore; on my feet were flat, clunky shoes that were big on me. I wore sunglasses and a masculine fedora that hid my dark, curly hair. In the mirror, I saw a heavy, crude, repulsive image that I had a hard time recognizing. In my pocket, I held a decree phrased in perfect German with the sign of the German eagle holding a swastika and the name of the local German authority, as well as a signature and a stamp. It was all made in our lab.

A taxi took me to the orphanage, which was in the old part of Grenoble, on a forested hill on the left bank of the river. When I arrived there, I ordered the driver to wait for me in a low voice and heavy German accent. I knocked on the carved wooden gate of the orphanage, and immediately I was caught up in my new character and felt no fear. When I entered, I took out the decree and demanded they hand over the baby. The caretakers scattered in every direction, while I stood in the dark corridor and waited for what seemed like forever.

"Where's the baby?" I yelled.

"She's still asleep," the matron said, and I saw the hate in her eyes.

"So wake her up!" I shouted, and glanced at my watch. It was already half past three, and the Gestapo people were liable to arrive any minute. The matron appeared and started telling me in detail the treatment the baby had received, when and what to feed her, and other things.

My patience had run out. "Enough with your nonsense!" I hollered, and slapped the matron. What all the shouting hadn't achieved, that slap in the face did. Within a second, I had the baby. I took her quickly, slammed the wooden gate behind me, and got into the taxi.

"To avenue Jean Jaures," I told the driver.

He left the tiny square and started driving toward the street, and then I noticed Thea and George following me on their bicycles. I realized they'd waited for me to make sure I left safely. I still had a long journey to Madame Jeanne's apartment ahead of me, where I was supposed to hand over the baby.

When we approached the tram station, I told the driver to stop. I got out of the taxi, took off the sunglasses and the hat, and opened the coat. I held Corinne as I waited for the tram to arrive. It was four when I boarded the tram, which was crammed with people. I was immediately given a place to sit. The pink baby with her round cheeks and ready smile unfortunately drew too much attention. It was only then that I thought about the sweet little creature in my arms.

To be on the safe side, I got off at the next station and walked the rest of the way. When I arrived at Madame Jeanne's apartment, I gave her the baby and left quickly, in case I was being followed. I was suddenly seized with a terrible lethargy, and the clunky shoes, which were too big on me, made it hard for me to walk. When I finally reached our room, I fell on the bed and felt neither joy nor pride that our mission had succeeded. Only complete emptiness.

***

How can I write about the MJS in Grenoble without mentioning the extraordinary Madame Jeanne, the woman to whom I'd brought the baby. Jeanne was twenty years older than us, a widow with two young boys. And yet she was an active participant in all our activities. She had fair hair and thick-lensed glasses through which innocent blue eyes stared. She was plump, and her generous breasts added to her maternal look. Where did she draw the patience and courage to take care of all those homeless people, feed dozens of hungry mouths when necessary?

She spoke French spiced with juicy Parisian slang and her typical humor, and she always, even when the situation was difficult, created a relaxed, optimistic atmosphere. The little house she rented on the outskirts of town was an old horse stable, and we felt the warmth of a real home there, which all of us missed.

But a respectful distance was always maintained. We called her Madame Jeanne. It was only natural that she take care of Corinne until we found the baby a foster family, who of course were unaware of her Jewish origins.

After this operation, it was obvious that the Gestapo would do everything in its power to capture the culprits. Grenoble wasn't a big city, and we feared that someone would recognize me. It was suggested that I dye my hair, but I rejected the idea. I was afraid to lose my confidence, because blonde hair would be in stark contrast to my appearance and draw attention.

At the end of the meeting, Sabine and I boarded the tram, and at one of the stations, German soldiers boarded. They spoke loudly about the abduction of a baby by an imposter who presented perfectly forged documents. "The brazenness of the Résistance has gone too far, but you can be sure that the Gestapo will catch them and know how to take care of them!"

There was no doubt that our operation had caused an uproar. We got off at the next station and walked the rest of the way. The two of us were deep in thought and wondered when the other shoe would drop, and it wasn't long before that happened. The manager of the orphanage knew Madeleine's address, and the Gestapo rushed over there, but this time, they were too late. Madeleine had left Grenoble right on time.

They didn't find a thing when they searched her apartment, but the landlady gave them the address of her younger sister, Simone. The Gestapo arrested and tortured her, but since she didn't know a thing, she couldn't give them the information they wanted. Simone was sent to Auschwitz and was murdered there. I never knew her, but for years, I was haunted by guilt that she paid with her life instead of me. Perhaps that was why, even after the war had ended, I never tried to find that baby. And on the rare occasions I mentioned the child's rescue story, I did so briefly and casually.

***

Years later, during the blazing summer season on an especially hot day in the Hula Valley, a dark, dusty car rolled into the kibbutz. Out of the car emerged four characters whom we weren't used to seeing in the area. There were two men wearing black jackets and black felt fedoras, while fringe peeked from beneath their shirts. With them came two women, who despite the heat wore dresses buttoned up to their necks with long sleeves that covered their arms. The kibbutz was empty. Most of the members were resting behind drawn shutters, waiting for the heat to slightly abate. The guests wandered about, asking about a "French woman named Renée," and received in response a bemused shrug. Luckily, they found a lone member in the secretariat who was just finishing for the day. Shulamit heard the words "French—Résistance—Renée" and brought them to me. I opened the door, sleep-dazed, and one of the women asked me excitedly, "Hello, are you Renée?" Without waiting for an answer, she added, "I'm Corinne, the baby you took from the orphanage in Grenoble. Do you remember?"

Thirty-four years had passed. Before me stood a young woman. Even her clumsy attire and the scarf that wouldn't let even one curl escape didn't detract from her beauty. I hugged Corinne and she clung to me.

Corinne told me her story.

> *I was still a little girl when I was told that the Gestapo wanted to take me from the orphanage but that someone from Grenoble's Résistance beat them to it, kidnapped me right beneath their noses, and saved me. It sounded like a fairy tale to me, and I wasn't sure if it was just a legend or if there was some truth in it. One day, I came across a book about the Jewish Résistance movement in France, and in it was the story of my rescue. I've been on edge ever since, searching for the people mentioned in the book. By chance, I met Rabbi Roitman in Jerusalem, Leon's brother, and from him I heard that you live on a kibbutz in the Galilee. So I've found you, after so many years.*

Corinne arrived in Lehavot HaBashan with her husband and the Martzbach family, both doctors, who were members of the Jewish orthodox community in Paris. She told me that after being moved from place to place, she came to their family at the age of fourteen, received in their home an orthodox upbringing, and immigrated with them to Israel. I told her she was a cheerful, pink-cheeked baby, and she couldn't get enough of hearing about herself. Together, we went to visit Madame Jeanne, who at the time lived in Jaffa. She, as always, welcomed us warmly with her juicy French and served us French dishes that were unfamiliar in Israel.

No one could know that several years later Corinne's husband would succumb to a disease and the Martzbach family would be killed in a car accident. Corinne married again and asked me to come to her wedding. "You're like a mother to me," she said. "You gave me my life."

***

In the spring and summer of 1944, the Germans had to retreat from many territories on the Russian front, territories that they occupied while suffering terrible casualties. In Italy, the Allies pushed them north after the terrible Battle of Monte Cassino, and Rome was liberated. At the beginning of June, the invasion of Normandy began, and Berlin and other cities in Germany were frequently bombed by the Allied air forces and partially destroyed.

I didn't know much about what was happening in the world, and once in a while, nuggets of information reached my ears. The only trustworthy source of information was Radio London, but few people had radios, and electricity was turned on for only two hours a day. Furthermore, the Germans disrupted broadcasting, making reception difficult. It was forbidden to listen to "the enemy's horrifying propaganda," and a person caught listening to it would be severely punished. There were many informants and collaborators willing to turn in those defying the ban to the German authorities.

My family was scattered: My father was in Poland, Bronia was somewhere in Belgium, Betty somewhere in Switzerland, and Mother in London. I even lost touch with La Hille and no longer knew if there were Jewish children there or if the place had been shut down and the children scattered all over. The handful of friends working with me in Grenoble were my entire world, but after the abduction, I was "burned," which meant I was no longer good for Résistance operations. We feared that the Gestapo was looking for me and that I could endanger not only myself, but my friends too. My friends demanded that I leave Grenoble and stop my underground activity.

At the time, the AJ planned to send groups of youngsters to Spain via the Pyrenees, and from there to Palestine. It was hinted that if I joined the AJ, they'd send me too. I didn't know then and still don't know who the members of the AJ were or their goals. I found the organization mysterious, and its active members were from Jewish high society and the Jewish intellectual strata in France. They were arrogant and detached from Judaism, and they supported Revisionist factions in Mandatory Palestine. All this was entirely opposed to my own views. But Henry IV, France's Protestant king, declared, "Paris is worth a Catholic Mass." And as far as I was concerned, the chance to immigrate to Palestine was worth swearing my allegiance to the AJ.

Thus, I found myself standing one afternoon in a busy street in Lyon, next to the main post office. In one hand, I held a women's magazine, and in the other, I held a pencil. Those were the signs by which I'd be recognized. I was supposed to wait for a man who would approach me with the question, "Damn, where is Republic Street?" and then follow him.

An hour passed. Each country has its customs. In France, a man wouldn't allow an attractive young girl to stand idly without offering his company for a little stroll or inviting her for an aperitif. I waved off several nuisances, and when a stranger arrived and said, "Damn, where is Republic Street?" I said a rude word and turned my back on him. The man passed by quickly and was swallowed in the crowd. There went my liaison.

Luckily, according to Résistance customs, another meeting was set for the next day, at the same place and time. The "Republic Street" man returned, and I followed him without catching a glimpse of his face. At the street corner, a car waited, and the man blindfolded me. The car ride seemed endless. Suddenly we stopped, and I was pushed out and then into a structure. There, my blindfold was removed and someone helped me down dark stairs that led to a basement. The door opened, and a strong shaft of light blinded me. Someone placed my hand on the Bible, which rested on a table covered with a blue-and-white flag. I sat facing a person whom I couldn't see, but perhaps there were two or three other people there. I was told to repeat the words of the oath, "I hereby swear to remain loyal to my country, the organization, and its officers."

The ceremony was over. Those present congratulated me and disappeared. Once again, someone blindfolded me, brought me to the car waiting on the street, and took me to a place where I spent the night. In the car, I received a briefing on how to meet "our person" in Toulouse, and then I was left alone. I replayed the ceremony again in my mind, which I thought was extremely ridiculous. I had no problem remaining loyal to my country and people, but I had no idea what the organization and officers, whom I was required to obey, stood for.

***

At the train station in Lyon, I recalled that cold gray morning at the beginning of 1943 when I first arrived with Lixie in the city, hoping that someone there would help us cross the border to Switzerland. We were penniless and had no documents, two young girls who for the first time left the children's home to go to an unfamiliar city. Could it be that only a year and a half had passed since? It seemed as though it happened so long ago. I was now the owner of an identity card of a real Frenchwoman, Renée Blanc, and in my pocket, I had money to sustain me. Even though the Gestapo was searching for me, I felt safe. At the station I met Paul, and I was surprised to hear that he was also on his way to Toulouse, to join the group that intended to cross the Pyrenees to Spain.

When we lived in Grenoble, Paul used to come to the

apartment I shared with Raymonde and enjoy our cooking. He was a sweet, born-and-bred Parisian, two years younger than me. His blond hair flopped on his forehead, and he had big, round blue eyes that stared at the world, making him look like a shy and innocent boy. I was glad that we were leaving together and had no idea that he was in love with me. I felt nothing more than motherly concern for him, which caused him great pain.

The train ride to Toulouse, which usually took about twelve hours, now took several days. When we boarded the train, we didn't know where it would stop, when it would derail because the tracks had been sabotaged, when the damage would be repaired, and from what town the train would make its way to the south. We walked part of the way, from town to town and from station to station. Every time, I was amazed anew at France's beauty. I said goodbye to the soft green hills, to the snowy mountains, to the raging streams, to the quaint villages with their picturesque churches. I inhaled the heavy fragrance of blooming flowers and the hay reaped in the fields. I thought about Israel, which I imagined as a hot, arid, desolate country filled with stones.

We walked for hours and were still a long way from Valence. From there, there were rumors that there was a train to Toulouse.

The roads were empty because the Germans confiscated most of the cars, so there was zero chance of catching a ride. Suddenly I saw a truck approaching and I waved to the driver, signaling that he stop. He did. I was amazed to see it packed with German soldiers. Paul recoiled, but I whispered, "Get on!

That's the best thing we can do. Who will think to search for Jews in this truck?"

I sat on a bench in the truck and looked around. Children wearing uniforms. How old were they? Sixteen at the most. Invincible Germany's situation must've been dire if it had to recruit such young boys. The discovery encouraged me, and when the truck stopped, we climbed off and continued walking.

The landscape changed. We were now in Provence, not far from Avignon. Olive and almond groves replaced the fields of crops. On the side of the road there were fig trees, and their unripe fruit gave off a spicy scent. The bridge at the entrance to Avignon was bombed. I remembered the words from a French children's song: "*Sur le pont d'Avignon, on y danse . . .*" (On the bridge of Avignon, there they dance . . .)

In Avignon, we entered an inn and were served squash and eggplant stew instead of the turnip soup of the north. A young French man joined us and ordered a local bottle of excellent wine, *Châteauneuf-du-Pape*. Fortified by the good food and wine, we continued. It wasn't long before we found out that Marcel—that was the name of the young man—was also headed to Toulouse. Marcel was a good-natured man, not especially smart, who didn't ask unnecessary questions as long as he consumed his daily quota of wine. I asked if he would like to join us because we were on our way to Toulouse and three were better than two. He was glad not to be alone, and I was glad that no one would suspect us now that we were in the company of a real Frenchman. Merry from the food and wine, Marcel started singing French marching songs, and we sang along with him.

And so we walked from town to town until we reached Nimes. From a distance, we noticed that the skies near our destination were covered with yellowish-gray fog, and as we moved closer to the city, we discovered its source. Nimes was brutally bombed by Allied bombers, and many houses had collapsed. The rubble of the houses blocked off entire streets. Hundreds of dead remained buried beneath the devastation, the bodies had started to rot, and the smell of death spread in the area. Many residents of the city found shelter between the mighty walls and arches of the Roman amphitheater, which had withstood the bombs.

We looked for a place to spend the night and luckily found a little hotel that remained intact.

"We have only one vacant room without water or electricity," we were told. We didn't hesitate and grabbed it. The boys gallantly went to sleep on the carpet, while I sprawled out in the double bed. In the morning, when I went down to reception to settle our bill, I was received with a cheerful "good morning" and a wink from all those present.

"Did you have a pleasurable night?" they asked.

It took some time until I understood what they meant.

"Yes," I said. "A wonderful night."

Those French, they managed to surprise me every time. Their city was half destroyed, many casualties were buried beneath the rubble, and they only had lustful thoughts in their minds.

***

We waited longer than expected in Toulouse while getting organized to cross the Spanish border. I found a temporary apartment on the ground floor of a building in a dubious part of the city. At night, men would make noise, knocking on the shutters of my window. They must've been clients of the previous tenant. They demanded that Dominique open the door.

I woke up early to escape the harassment and wandered along the city streets. I remember that on the theater building, a beautiful neoclassical structure, there had been posters announcing a concert conducted by Bruno Walter. It seemed ironic, that combination of war and culture.

In the markets, throngs of German soldiers searched for presents for their wives or mistresses back home. It was strange to think that they too had mothers, sisters, and sweethearts. French merchants overpriced and profited twice; they made money and also cheated the hated "*Boches*."

I searched the market for a pair of stout leather boots that would endure the hike in the mountains. However, the only thing I found in the shops were cloth sandals with soles made out of rope, or fashionable shoes with cork wedges. Neither one was appropriate for the journey. Finally, I found a shoemaker far from the city center, in a gloomy alcove, and there I found what I wanted: high boots made of leather with real leather soles.

***

But that wasn't where the story ended. In Spain, in the city of Lerida, we passed by a procession of women prisoners who were opposed to Franco's regime. They were on their way to a day of forced labor and walked by wearing only rags on their feet. The moment the guards' attention was elsewhere, my friends and I threw our shoes toward them.

On my last day in Toulouse, I felt full of mischief. On the banks of the river Garonne, which split the town, there was a boat marina. I had never sailed in a boat, but it seemed like a safe and enjoyable pastime, so I rented a boat for two hours. One of the marina workers pushed me to the middle of the river. The current took me effortlessly. It was a clear day, and the sun reflected in thousands of sparkles on the water. I sat, holding the oars, and succumbed to the pleasure of rowing a boat all by myself for the first time in my life.

Suddenly the bow of the boat got stuck in a tangle of vegetation and sandbank in the middle of the river. I'd run into a small island and had a difficult time extracting myself. I tried for some time but was unsuccessful. Suddenly I heard laughter and cheering from above. I raised my head and saw a bridge overhead and a crowd of curious onlookers who were enjoying the free show. The last thing I needed was all the attention. Making a supreme effort, I dug the oar in the sand and extracted myself as the crowd above cheered and applauded. The adventure ended when my two hours were up.

That was my last day in Toulouse. I planned to travel to Carcassonne the next day, and from there board the train that would bring me to a town near the Spanish border. I took advantage of the hours I had until my next train to visit the old part of the city, which maintained a medieval style. Carcassonne was surrounded by an impressive wall. I entered it via the large gate and roamed the winding alleys among the old houses. Signs made by artisans declared their owners' professions: large scissors indicated a tailor, a shoe a shoemaker, every profession and its symbol. At a time when most of the population didn't know how to read or write, these signs were extremely important. The streets were empty, and I wandered about dreamily, for a while forgetting the circumstances that brought me there.

***

Dozens of years later, I visited Carcassonne again. Many tourists roamed its narrow alleys, ate in the restaurants opened in the old houses, and in the evenings, enjoyed its bars and nightclubs. Carcassonne had changed, but when I circled the walls again on the pebble-paved road surrounding the town, far from the bustling crowd, I felt that same long-ago magic.

***

In the afternoon, I boarded a train that brought me to a godforsaken town called Quillan. When we arrived, a handful of locals got off as well as several young men and women, myself among them. They looked around, as though searching for something.

At the end of the platform stood a sturdy man wearing a black Basque hat. He waved and quickly left the station. The group of youngsters and I followed him.

It wasn't long before our small group of eight was making its way through tangled green vegetation and low shrubs, following the Spanish border smuggler. Trampled weeds were the only things indicating we were walking on some sort of path. We walked quickly up a moderate incline, and I started sweating. The rucksack on my back was heavy, and my feet still weren't used to my new shoes.

After two silent hours of climbing through the thicket, the Spaniard gave us a ten-minute break. I dropped down and wasn't sure I would be able to get up and continue, and if I'd even have the strength to cross the Pyrenees if I was so tired after such a short hike. The guide's voice interrupted my thoughts. "Now put all the documents, photos, letters, and other unnecessary scraps of paper in a pile!"

The Spaniard piled dry twigs around the papers and lit them. A pile ignited and then extinguished quickly, and he covered the ashes with earth. That was the end of my "legitimate" identification document. The last pictures of my parents and sisters were also consumed by the fire. I was now a nameless person without a past. Just for a moment, I regretted giving everything up so easily and giving in to the tempting adventure called Spain in order to immigrate to Israel.

I recalled the book *The Death Ship* by the German writer Traven, which Eugen Lyrer read to us every evening before we went to sleep. It was about a man who lacked documentation of citizenship after World War I, and without it, it was as though he'd never existed.

The hike in the mountains continued, with five-minute breaks every hour. It was extremely difficult to continue after that short break. At the time, I didn't know that only two weeks before, a large group on their way to Spain were caught. Among those caught were two active members of the organization arranging the crossing into Spain: Leon Cohen, the brother of Haim Cohen who would later become a Supreme Court judge in Israel, and Jacques Roitman, the brother of Aryeh and Paul Roitman from MJS. The Germans found a bag with a prayer book and phylacteries in Leon's rucksack. He was sent to Auschwitz and never returned. Jacques had excellent French papers. He was sent as a Frenchman to mandatory labor in Germany. After the war, he returned to Paris. The Spanish guide, who tried to escape, was shot. Our guide had many reasons to hurry us and stay away from populated settlements.

In the evening, we arrived at a Maquis stronghold, which was set up in a deserted flour mill and in several other temporary structures. Sloppily dressed bearded men with rifles hanging from their shoulders surrounded us curiously. They didn't look like daring freedom fighters but rather like a ragtag band of outlaws. It seemed as though women hadn't visited the stronghold for quite a while, so the few girls in our group received an enthusiastic welcome. To my surprise, I found among the group that arrived before us Henri and Ilse from La Hille. That evening, Ilse and I sat with the "warriors," who poured us glass after glass of wine and cognac. Ilse was lucky enough to sit by the wall next to a thirsty plant, into which she poured the alcohol. I took advantage of every minute of distraction and poured the wine beneath the table. Our hosts never noticed as they were extremely drunk and admired our drinking prowess. Their heads fell on the table, and we could finally leave the table, go to the flour mill, and get some sleep. We shut all the windows and barricaded the door with whatever we could find. We also stationed guards, fearing the drunken men would try to surprise us.

It was still dark when they woke us up in the morning. The members of our little group gathered around two tables, and the only woman in the stronghold served us bean porridge. She looked old before her time, wearing a black dress like the peasants in the area, her hair faded, her mouth pursed, her expression severe. She moved among the tables and served us a large portion of beans with strips of pork still covered with bristles. The two young men who sat with me at the table were religious and pushed the plate away in revulsion. However, the guide, who noticed that, ordered them to eat and, after an argument, said decisively, "If you won't eat, you're not coming with me."

The two young men had an agitated consultation and, in the end, pulled their plates closer and started eating. I struggled with my plate and tried to swallow the pieces of pork fat without chewing so as not to taste their disgusting texture.

***

The Pyrenees Mountains are a natural border between France and Spain and run from the Mediterranean in the east to the Atlantic in the west, about 500 kilometers. They are 3,400 meters high. On the French side, the mountain slopes are steep and it's difficult to cross. When closer to the coast, the passes are easy and there are paved roads.

When we left, another man, a young Spaniard, joined our guide. After a short walk, the electricity poles disappeared and we didn't see a hut, tree, or path—not even sheep or goat dung, indicating that shepherds took their herds here. We climbed up and down hills and saw only sparse gray weeds everywhere we looked. I wondered how the guides could find their way in this desolate landscape.

Two days later, the terrain became extremely rocky. We carefully jumped from rock to rock. There were rumors that in one of the previous groups, one of the men broke his leg, thus sealing his fate. There was no way to help him continue, and he asked to be shot so he wouldn't fall prey to the wild animals.

We must've reached a high altitude because there was deep snow in the crevices and there were areas covered with slippery ice. Once every so often, someone would ask the guides, "When will we get there?" and a guide would answer, "Soon. You see that hill there? We'll climb it and that's it." But we already knew that behind the ridge he pointed to would be another ridge and then another one.

We walked only at night. During the day, we hid. At the end of the third day, we ran out of food, and the only thing left was several kilos of sugar cubes. Our destination seemed so far away. Had our guides lost their way? We feared that they would abandon us in the mountains. Our blood, Jewish blood, was cheap.

We appointed two men to distribute the remaining sugar three times a day, two sugar cubes per person. We drank from the water streams and the accumulated snow, which tasted wonderful. I didn't drink the snow as much as I ate it, and I discovered in it all the flavors of the world. If I wanted, the snow tasted like a fresh roll with butter, or a yeast cake during the Sabbath, or a banana or a pineapple. That was probably the taste of the manna the Israelites ate in the desert.

One morning, after a hard night of walking, we rested by a small lake in the mountains, its waters crystal clear. I sprawled in the grass, dozing. Maybe it was because of the thin mountain air, the bone-deep exhaustion, and the lack of food, but suddenly I thought of a poem by Schiller, a famous German poet. Liberally translated, these were the sentences I thought of: "The lake smiles, beckoning for a dip. The boy falls asleep in the green grass . . ."

I yearned to stay there forever, and felt as though I were fading away and nothing was important. I didn't feel hunger or pain, only a desire to blend with surroundings. It was a wonderful feeling.

Tensions arose between some of the men and the guides. The men went to the guides and complained that there was no food. They expressed their suspicion that the guides had food. In response, the guides emptied their rucksacks, and we saw socks, woolen vests, a bottle of cognac, a flashlight, and two hand grenades. That action was worth more than a thousand words.

I lost track of the days. One dark starless, moonless night, we walked silently in a column. Suddenly I noticed that I could no longer see the person in front of me. It was forbidden to shout, and in the darkness, I tried to make out the person walking before me, but to no avail. I started climbing toward where I assumed everyone had gone, and when I stopped for a minute to breathe, I discovered that six people were following me. While I walked to catch up with the rest, someone thumped me on my back, and a flashlight blinded me. The guide had noticed that several people were missing. How had he managed to find us in that darkness? I have no doubt that he saved our lives.

The next night, we received a special briefing before crossing the road that signaled the border between France and Andorra. The road was illuminated with spotlights, and German soldiers patrolled it. Each one of us had to cross the road by turns and roll several meters down the steep incline on the other side. We did as instructed until all of us crossed safely, and we continued walking until we arrived at a fast-flowing river. The guides told us that the bank on the other side was in Andorra's jurisdiction. We took off our shoes and entered the water, which came up to our waists and was breathtakingly cold. The guides helped us cross safely, making sure that the current wouldn't sweep us away.

Finally, we reached Andorra, a country where nothing could hurt us. But the journey's hardships hadn't ended yet. There were still quite a few hills to climb. At dawn, I saw a figure standing on a hill, raising her face to the sky, her arms over her head as though she were praying, and I heard her shout, "This is where I'm staying. I'm not going to take even one more step!"

No, it wasn't a mistake. It was Ilse. The guide walked up to her and said, "You're not staying here. You're going," and slapped her. "Are you going?" Another ringing slap and Ilse snapped out of it. Her arms dropped, and the guide tied a rope around her body and held on to the end. That was how she followed him until we saw the first sign of settlement, which was an empty cabin. From there, we still had a couple of hours to walk until we reached Andorra. I don't remember the names or faces of the people with whom I crossed the Pyrenees, only the sight of Ilse on top of that hill, and Henri, protecting his violin like a mother protected her baby.

***

In 1999, Dadi and I went on a tour of Scandinavia. In the bus, I heard someone speaking Hebrew with a French accent. I introduced myself and found out that the man had immigrated to Israel from France, through Spain. He told me that when his group crossed the Pyrenees, they had no food left, only a small number of sugar cubes that he was in charge of distributing. Two sugar cubes three times a day to each member. Apparently, we'd shared that journey.

***

I'll never forget our elation when we gathered in the hotel's dining room in Andorra. Our exhaustion seemed to disappear. Dirty, with torn clothes and blistered hands and feet, we stood straight and sang the national anthem, "Hatikvah," at the top of our lungs.

Our Spanish guides looked at us in bemusement, not understanding the change that had come over us. They probably didn't know or feel the weight that had slid off our shoulders. We were drunk with victory. We felt we had overcome all our hardships and had received another lease on life. We indulged. In the hotel restaurant, we were served hot, filling soup, and in the basement, there were stone pools with warm water from the springs. I dipped into the water, scrubbing off the filth that had clung from the journey. It was still early, but I went up to my room to lie down. When I woke up, it was dark. Unbelievably, I'd slept for twenty-four hours straight.

***

Andorra is a small, independent enclave, hidden among the high cliffs of the Pyrenees, an odd remnant from medieval times, like Monaco and Lichtenstein. In 1944, Andorra had a population of fifty-five hundred. The people spoke Catalan, as in the north of Spain, but the official languages were French and Spanish. The entire city was built along one street, the houses on both sides hidden among the huge boulders. In the evening, colorful street lights went on in the cafés and the many bars, which played cheerful music. New cars, the likes of which we hadn't seen in France for a long time, parked on the side of the road. Andorra had always been a smugglers' paradise. One could get, tax-free, all the merchandise that was scarce in France. The guides invited the girls of the group to a night out, and we celebrated until the early morning hours.

We took advantage of the few days we had left in Andorra to visit the radio station. The broadcasts from Andorra were well known all over occupied Europe. The station broadcast reliable news about the war, beautiful folk songs, updates on the current fashions, and commercials that were popular in France and Europe. I was surprised to see that all this came out of a small, modest studio. The team welcomed us warmly, and we told them how popular they were on the other side of the mountains.

***

Nowadays, many tourists visit Andorra to buy tax-free products. I visited there in 1988 and was sorry to see the huge billboards advertising cigarettes and alcohol blemishing the landscape. Gone were the stone benches around the warm-water spring pools at the end of the street. Gone also were the women who would wash their laundry with wide wooden paddles while chattering gaily.

Ruth

SPANISH FIESTA

Several days later, we took a car to Spain and reached a border town just before midnight. I assume our arrival was known of in advance, because in spite of the late hour, a large crowd of curious onlookers was waiting for us. We entered the border police's hut yet weren't required to show documents or permits, which we didn't have. Our arrival and entrance had been settled beforehand. The only thing checked was the content of our rucksacks.

I entered the hut, and the policemen started exclaiming, "*Guapa, guapa, muy guapa.*" (Beautiful, beautiful, very beautiful.) With their strange three-cornered hats, these policemen looked like actors in the "*comedia del arte.*" They went through what few belongings I had in my rucksack, and with that, the check was over. When I returned to the car, I discovered that the silver pen I'd received for my birthday from my friends in Grenoble had been taken as a "souvenir."

After the border check, we continued to Lleida, where we met the members of the Dutch group who, like us, arrived in Spain after a rigorous journey. Now the *apatridos* (the people with no country) filled up two hotels in that little town. Lleida still had damage from the civil war: pits in the roads, half-ruined houses, bumpy pavement, and terrible poverty. Families lived beneath bridges, where they cooked, washed, and raised their children. Gangs of abandoned children, in which the oldest couldn't be more than twelve and the youngest five or six, roamed the city and found shelter in derelict structures. Almost every day, there was a street procession headed by priests; behind them a life-sized statue of the Madonna or Jesus was carried, and behind that, men carrying candles walked while singing and ringing bells. The smell of incense was heavy in the air.

I find it important to mention that Franco's Spain didn't turn in Jews to the Germans or prevent them from entering the country. Officially, all male refugees between the ages of eighteen and forty were supposed to be sent to a detention camp, but the Spanish weren't strict about the matter and it was enough to declare, "I'm seventeen and a half," or "I'm over forty," in order to gain freedom.

With our arrival in Lleida, we received money to buy cloth to sew a nice suit. After all, we had to appear in the hotel and on the streets dressed appropriately. Those were the conditions that the Spanish government agreed upon with the "Joint." Apart from hotel accommodations and three meals per day, each of us received a weekly allowance for personal expenses, thus freeing us from financial worries during those months until we immigrated to Palestine.

***

The Dutch group was a close-knit one. Most of them were members of Zionist Youth Movements from Germany who stayed in Holland in training farms. Their journey from Holland to France and from there to Spain is just one of the many examples of Jews finding a way to survive.

The German organization "Todt" recruited laborers for construction work for the German Army. The Dutch were considered part of the Aryan race and received senior positions within the organization. The fair-haired and blue-eyed members of the group joined Todt as Dutch citizens, and it wasn't long before they held key positions. Later on, they recruited other members from the training group for the organization, provided them with documents that helped them move freely about occupied Europe, and also managed to contact the Jewish underground members of AJ. Without a doubt, these were daring and resourceful men who managed to save themselves and their friends.

One of those men was Martin, whom I'd heard of when I was still in France. Raymonde, my friend and roommate, met him once during one of the Résistance operations, and he immediately became her Prince Charming. She talked about him endlessly, and according to her description, there was no other man like him in terms of beauty, wisdom, and gentleness.

When I found out Martin was in Lleida, my curiosity was

piqued and I wanted to meet him. We talked and talked and talked and became close. He was ten years older than me, calm and very practical. He helped me with all the initial matters that I had to take care of, and I saw him as a father figure or a big brother whom I could consult with and rely on. Martin never participated in all the passionate arguments that the other group members had about socialism, communism, the national kibbutz movement or the united kibbutz movement, religion, or the observation of the commandments. Yet his reserve never stopped me from participating.

In Lleida, the Dutch initiated cultural events with us and organized Hebrew and geography lessons. We published a daily newsletter, *The Lleida Page*, and on Friday evenings we held social events. I knew German and French and had nice handwriting, so I was busy editing and copying local items and various articles.

None of us knew when and where the ship to Palestine would set sail from. There was no one to ask, but that didn't really bother me. I was free of worries, I ate plentifully, and I enjoyed the company of people I liked. It was a break between years of fleeing and hiding and fear before building a new life.

***

At the beginning of June, the Allied Forces landed in Normandy, made their way to Paris, and defeated the Germans time after time. At the end of August, Paris was liberated, the Germans retreated, and France was freed. We received this encouraging news much later, and we didn't know that the fighting in the east was continuing and would continue for many more months. The Nazi murdering machine upped its output, and many more Jews would die a terrible death until the final victory over the Germans in May 1945.

In the meantime, in Lleida, youthful energy overflowed. After years of misery, we were filled with a desire to rejoice and enjoy as much as possible. When we heard of a religious festival in one of the villages, we would go there, even though sometimes it was a two-hour walk or more. Each village had its own saint, and each saint had his or her day of the year. We went from fiesta to fiesta, sometimes twice a week.

In the village square, colorful lights shone brightly, a small orchestra played music, and the stalls offered sweets and drinks. Children of all ages ran around until the wee hours of the morning. We were invited to join the dancing. If a boy wanted to invite a girl to dance, he'd hand her a basket full of flowers and sweets. The girl who responded to his invitation hung the basket on her arm. Ilse and I were given many baskets. We danced, went crazy, and laughed and laughed. We were also offered countless cups of wine, but we were careful and emptied the cups beneath the table. On the other hand, we never refused the ice cream we were offered, much to our hosts' amusement.

One night, a merry group of us sat and we mentioned that we were on our way to Mandatory Palestine. The Spanish men were astounded. "What do girls like you have in remote, desolate, and hot *Palestina*? Stay in Spain. Before long, you'll find a handsome man, marry him, and live a wonderful life."

A man wearing a fancy suit said to us, "If we're talking about Palestine, I have an offer you can't refuse. I'm in the fire extinguishing business, and I assume that there's no shortage of fires in a hot, dry country. I want you to represent my company in Palestine."

We laughed because his offer seemed crazy. But the strange thing is that my kibbutz, Lehavot HaBashan, has a factory that manufactures equipment to extinguish fires.

***

I ate well in Lleida, but I was eager for variety, for more food. When some guys took a handful of almonds out of their pockets, cracked them with a stone, and offered them to everyone, I wanted to know how they got them.

"Easy!" they said. "The entire area is full of almond orchards. All you have to do is collect the almonds that fall from the tree."

The next day, I left with my friends to raid the almond orchards near the city. The sun had just risen, and it was still cool. We walked for almost an hour. As the day drew on, it got warmer, and we reached an orchard bordering the road. Here and there we saw breaches in the fence through which we entered, and then we scattered around the orchard.

I had a shoulder bag. I started collecting the almonds, enjoying the protective shade of the trees. My bag filled quickly, and I was so busy collecting the almonds that I didn't notice someone approaching. Suddenly, a muscular man stood before me wearing work clothes, boots, and a cap shading his eyes.

Without a word, he took my bag and signaled that I follow him. Images flashed through my mind, each one scarier than the last. He'd turn me in to the police, they'd arrest me, they'd throw me in jail or worse! Perhaps they'd deport me to the other side of the border. I wondered where everyone else was. Had they been caught as well? And why was the man silent and not yelling at me?

I obediently followed the man into the orchard, and we arrived at a place where the laborers were collecting almonds. Without a word, the man signaled that I join them and start collecting. I worked from morning till evening, drank diluted wine with the laborers, and ate with them when they took a break. When darkness fell, the man gave me back my rucksack. I thanked him shamefacedly. The man was smart and had made his point.

***

Several weeks passed, and we moved from Lleida to Barcelona, where we lived in small groups in various places, so it was difficult to continue the social events we'd held in Lleida. Mostly, we met at the city's central boulevard, which we had christened "*Boulevard des Apatridos.*" In the evening, we'd walk up and down the boulevard and pass the time arguing endlessly about matters of the world and guessing whether we'd set sail to Palestine while the war still raged on. Friendships formed, and love bloomed . . . and wilted.

As the High Holidays approached, our religious members

tried to obtain permission to rent a hall in order to pray, and the unbelievable happened: The Spanish authorities gave us their permission to rent a place in order to conduct public prayer. I remembered what my father had told me, that the Jews had declared a boycott on Spain ever since the expulsion. The Spanish authorities' permission was no laughing matter, as the Jewish expulsion decree from 1492 was still valid and ended only in 1968. After Hitler's rise to power, several thousand Jews found asylum in Spain as individuals but weren't permitted to establish a community. In Spain, Catholicism was exclusive and no other religion was permitted.

I took part in the New Year and Yom Kippur prayers. Although I no longer observed the commandments, and I'd also lost my faith in God, the familiar prayer songs took me back to my childhood, to the days I accompanied my father to the synagogue.

I remembered them, and it filled me with yearning.

***

Several days after the Jewish New Year, we were invited to the British Consulate in Barcelona to settle the matter of our entrance permit to Palestine, that same certificate that my father was denied. I still have the letter from 1938, signed by the High Commissioner for Palestine, that rejected my father's request. Our family history could have been so different if only we'd received a positive answer!

I viewed this invitation as a sign that the date of my

immigration was approaching, and that evening, when I said goodbye to Martin, I was in high spirits. We agreed to make the most of the days we had left in Barcelona and familiarize ourselves with the beautiful city. However, in the end, I didn't see a thing and remember little of my stay there. When I arrived at my room, I found a letter from the British Consulate. The consulate was "pleased to announce that following the request of Mrs. Schütz, [I would be] permitted to immigrate to England." They added that because of the war, they didn't know when I'd be able to make the journey. I had to travel to Lisbon and contact the British Consulate there.

I was amazed. How had my mother managed to overcome British bureaucracy and get me the permit so quickly? She herself was a refugee who barely made a living working in a uniform factory in bombed London.

For the first time, I had two entirely different options and I had to choose. External circumstances that I had no control over no longer navigated my life. Now I was the one to decide my future. I didn't sleep for three nights. I was extremely agitated. Should I immigrate to Israel and realize my dream, or travel to London and join my mother? Five and a half years had passed since that cold and gloomy day in February 1939, the day I left Berlin, and I could still see my mother waving goodbye, running down the platform until the train left the station. I missed her terribly. I wanted to see her and be with her after so many years of separation. On the other hand, all those years I'd clung to the hope that one day I'd immigrate to Israel, and that day was indeed approaching.

What should I do? Should I travel to England, help my mother bring Betty and Bronia back, and help her make a living? As for my father, I didn't believe he was alive, and I assumed my mother was deluding herself, expecting him to return from the inferno. What a terrible blow it would be when she found out he wasn't coming back. I couldn't leave her alone or disappoint her. But on the other hand, could I turn my back on my beliefs? Didn't I have obligations beyond my family? Would I continue living my life in the diaspora?

I should mention that the entrance permit was a single-entry immigration permit for a specifically scheduled voyage from Spain.

I had no choice. First I had to go to London, to my mother, and after some time, I'd immigrate to Israel. But the chance to receive a new certificate was almost nil, and I doubted I'd manage to get the money for traveling expenses.

After a long and restless night, the day of my visit to the consulate dawned. When I woke up, my head was heavy, and all the way to the consulate, I continued deliberating with myself without reaching a decision. At the building's entrance, I hesitated for a second, and suddenly my feet carried me, of their own volition, to the office in charge of passengers to Palestine. That was it. I had decided. It was as though an invisible force had decided for me. The agony of indecision was over, and a sweet calmness came over me. I was on my way to Israel to realize my dream.

That day, I wrote my mother a long letter, trying to explain what caused me to choose to immigrate to Israel instead of joining her in England. I tried to find the right words that would ease the blow, and emphasized that my decision hadn't been easy and didn't stem from insensitivity. I loved her and missed her and knew how hard it was for her to be separated from her daughters.

But our people, the Jewish people, had suffered a terrible devastation. Many had been murdered, and I, who'd survived, felt it was my responsibility to invest all my efforts in the national goal, to do something so that we too would have our own country. I didn't want to exchange one diaspora with another, I concluded. "I'm sure, Mutti," I wrote, "that you wouldn't want me to walk around for the rest of my life feeling as though I were missing something. And if I come to England, that is certainly what will happen."

I also wrote that I hoped it wouldn't be long before Betty and Bronia came to her, and then the three of them would come to Israel and live with me. Today, these words may seem pompous and full of pathos, but at the time, they expressed exactly what I thought and felt—me and many others.

It took Mother another five years to save enough money so she could visit me in Israel, and another five years passed until I had the means to travel to London and stay there for an entire month. I felt, once again, as though I were my mother's little girl, and I saw, for the first time in years, my sisters, whom I hadn't seen since the war.

When she visited Israel and the kibbutz, my mother was deeply shocked by our difficult living conditions. At the time, we lived in a tiny room in a wooden shack with no running water. The water faucet was in the yard, and a tin hut with a hole in the ground served as the outhouse. During the day, the sun blazed on the black basalt stones, and the heat was relentless. All day long, clouds of mosquitoes harassed us.

Every Saturday evening, I'd write a letter to my mother, and every week I received a letter from her. She never expressed any resentment over my preference to immigrate to Israel, and she never criticized the life I'd chosen. However, long after her first visit, she told me that she hadn't stopped crying every time she remembered my living conditions.

She broke her silence only one time, and that was during those tense, nerve-wracking days before the Six-Day War. I received an urgent letter from her in which she wrote, "Send the children to England immediately. I've taken care of everything. It's bad enough that you're crazy, but for God's sake, have mercy on the children! Send them at once!" My mother, who at the time had to send us beyond the border without knowing what would become of us and in doing so saved our lives, had the right to demand that from me.

I replied, "Mutti, until now I've run from one place to the other, from country to country. We're done running. The children are staying with us, no matter what happens. Let's hope for the best."

***

Let's return to Spain. After completing all the official arrangements in Barcelona, we traveled to the port city of Cadiz. The journey was tedious. We passed through monotonous landscape: dry, arid earth, barren fields after the harvest. I hoped we'd stop in Madrid and visit, but the train skipped the city and stopped at miserable, godforsaken places.

Little girls wearing long, filthy dresses greeted us at those stations and competed among themselves to sell us water. They were dirty, and their hair hadn't seen a comb in ages. Yelling and begging, they extended their thin arms toward us, holding cups of water poured from clay jars. This picture repeated itself in every station, and the poverty in those places is seared in my mind as a horrifying thing. I wondered if it was the Spanish Civil War that had brought the Spanish people so low, or was this the situation beforehand and now it had just deteriorated? I felt lucky and even ashamed, because the Jewish people had so generously helped us through the Joint.

It's strange, but I don't remember whether there were any local passengers apart from us on the train. The only thing I remember is our car. I guess I fell asleep on a hard bench, and when I woke up, we were already close to our destination.

Cadiz is an old city on the west side of the Strait of Gibraltar, an enclave on the Atlantic Ocean. It was built by one of Hannibal's descendants, and some claim that the source of the town's name is "Kadesh" ("holy" in Hebrew). Our group was put up in a big hotel outside the city. The hotel walls bordered the sea, and it was the first time I came across the natural phenomenon of ebb and flow, which fascinated me. I tirelessly followed the sea's withdrawal and discovered the wide plains revealed. Shells and shellfish remained on the beach, giving off a powerful smell, and the revealed territory was like an ideal playing field. We played ball and raced each other. And in the evening, the sea covered everything. When the tide was high, the waves crashed against the hotel wall.

It wasn't hot here like it was in Lleida. We enjoyed the clear, sunny days of autumn. I roamed the city with Martin. I loved the purple bougainvillea, which were a stark contrast to the white houses that were one- or two-stories high. We visited the churches, the beautiful cathedrals, we saw the ancient Roman remains, and we sat in the shade of the trees in the cafés. Andalusia's laid-back atmosphere charmed me, and I abandoned the heavy, suffocating clothes of the north. I bought some faux silk material—red with white polka dots—and made myself a long wide skirt like the Andalusian women wore.

On the street corners stood wagons that sold thin strips of deep-fried dough sprinkled with sugar in paper bags. We'd nibble on them as we walked, chattering and laughing, sometimes planning for the future. I especially grew fond of a certain type of halva that almost made me miss the ship leaving Cadiz.

Before boarding the ship, we stood in a long line, waiting to have our documents checked by the harbor police. I thought that it would be a while before Martin's and my turn and I'd have enough time to buy that heavenly sweet. Martin, unexpectedly, gave in to my foolery. It was noon, the siesta time, and all the shops were closed. Hoping to find an open kiosk, I continued searching until we found halva. But when we returned with our treasure to the port, the platform was empty. Everyone was on the ship, the two policemen holding our papers were just preparing to leave, and the sailors were preparing to raise the gangplank. Sheepish and shamefaced, we boarded the ship at the last minute.

***

The Jewish Agency in Lisbon rented the *Guinea*. When it arrived at Cadiz, it already held a group of children gathered from occupied Europe. We set sail on October 26, 1944, and reached Tangier the next day, where several Jewish families boarded the ship. All in all, we numbered three hundred passengers. We crossed the Mediterranean from the west side, through the Strait of Gibraltar to the east side, and within ten days, we arrived at Haifa. On the night we set sail, we held an assembly on deck in memory of all the people who had perished, said goodbye to cursed Europe, and sang "Hatikvah." After everyone scattered, I stood for a long time on the deck, looking at the waves crashing against the bow of the ship. I was too excited to sleep.

The *Guinea* sailed under the flag of neutral Portugal, and despite the war, the journey passed without a hitch. The weather during this season was stormy, and the ship was old and small. Many of us, myself included, were seasick. When the sea calmed somewhat and I felt my legs were steady, I went down below to the kitchen and machine rooms. The kitchen was tiny and airless and stunk horribly. Next to the boilers stood a half-naked sweaty stoker who seemed to be engulfed by red flames. That's how I imagined hell and the Devil, fanning the flames of the inferno. I was horrified to see the awful conditions people had to endure in order to make a living.

MY FIRST ORANGE IN ISRAEL

Nine days after we set sail, we noticed land through the early morning mist.

"*Palestina a la vista*!" (you can see Palestine) one of the sailors yelled. We rushed excitedly to the deck. Two of His Majesty's police boats sailed out to meet us. The sailors lowered a ladder, and the policemen climbed up and started methodically checking everyone's papers. This was our first meeting with the foreign reign in Israel. The next day, the ship docked at the Port of Haifa. We were still on the ship when photographers from the local paper rushed to the port and, in Yiddish, urged us to sing the national anthem. At the time, news reels were presented in the cinema before every movie.

I studied the people standing on the dock, trying to find the representative of the organization to which I had sworn my alliance in Lyon before the crossing to Spain. I was afraid that the organization would demand that I join their ranks, but my fears were groundless. No one came to demand that I fulfill my oath.

A row of buses stood before the port. I stood there, holding an orange in one hand and my little suitcase containing all my worldly possessions in the other, and naïvely thought we'd travel straight to Haifa. I was mistaken. After a short distance, the bus stopped next to a double barbed-wire fence and watchtowers. We'd arrived at the detention camp in Atlit. Policemen wearing high fur hats greeted us, but this wasn't the welcome I'd wished for.

In the camp, there was a row of wooden barracks where the internees lived, and tin structures served as the dining room. Along the walls in the barracks stood beds covered with prickly wool blankets. I lived with the women who boarded the ship in Tangier. They seemed to me extremely exotic and intriguing. They had lush bodies and wore colorful dresses. On their arms, they had many bangles, and they sat cross-legged and at ease on their beds and chatted among themselves in a strange language. They were busy with their own matters and didn't notice me or even say hello. I felt uncomfortable, as though I'd entered their territory without permission. After all, they were the descendants of the Jews exiled from Spain, whom I'd heard so much about. I was Jewish and they were Jewish, so why were we so different?

In Atlit, for the first time I met Jews who had escaped the death camps and arrived in Israel after hair-raising journeys. They went through the seven stations of hell and told us horrifying stories. Compared to them, we were spoiled, which, for example, was expressed in our table manners. Before mealtime, we'd wait quietly for the doors of the dining room to open, but the survivors of the camps burst inside the minute the doors opened, shoved us aside, and snatched everything they could. And then they were on their way out again, to the second dining room. The quick ones even made it to the third one. We didn't stand a chance and couldn't compete with them.

We were provided with an endless supply of bread and margarine, and grapefruits as well. By the way, grapefruit was not a known fruit in Europe and many of the internees tried to eat the grapefruit like one eats an orange. But the bitterness repulsed them, and they never touched it again.

Many organizations helped improve the internees' conditions in Atlit. I remember a piece of laundry soap imprinted with the word or name "Shemen." I weighed the soap in my hand, smelled it, and delighted in it. I hurried to the taps in the yard and started washing my underclothes, loving the velvety white foam of real soap that I hadn't had for years.

A year later, in the laundromat in the kibbutz, a piece of soap fell into a tub of water. The laundress didn't bother fishing it out, but instead took a new piece of soap and continued laundering. I imagined that soap dissolving, and at lunch, I snuck to the tub, dipped my hand into the water, and "saved" that precious piece of soap.

The weather changed, and it rained endlessly for days. The camp became muddy, and rivulets of brown water ran through it. My little cardboard suitcase got wet and crumbled. I bundled my possessions in one of the two shirts I owned. That day, I received a message from my uncle Max through an acquaintance who worked in the camp. Max asked how he could help me, and two days later, he sent me a new suitcase containing the most precious thing: a pair of rubber boots. I had them for years.

The first group released from the camp was the group of children and their escorts and mothers with babies. After some time, it was finally my turn. I was summoned to headquarters. A British officer sat behind a large desk, offered me a seat, and started interrogating me thoroughly. Among other things, he asked me when and how I left Germany and what I had done in France. When he heard my answers, he was thoughtful for some time, and then asked again, as though trying to confuse me and find contradictions in my story. Eventually, he was convinced that I was indeed a Jewish refugee from Germany and not a spy. And then he started writing my name, where I was born and on what date, and other things I told him on a lengthy sheet of paper with my passport photo. I had a brief thought that I could've given him whatever name I wanted, invented anything about my identity, and he would've documented everything.

With my new document, I went to the Jewish agency's headquarters. Behind a long table sat several clerks, and when one of them heard I had a family in Israel and I wanted to meet them, he quickly handed me over to another clerk in case I had regrets and needed his help. The other clerk gave me a sum of money that was just enough to bring me to Jerusalem, and a third clerk gave me papers stating I was a new immigrant and was entitled to an iron bed, a seaweed-stuffed mattress, and a blanket.

After presenting all my documents, the guards opened the inner gate of Atlit camp, several steps away from the outer gate. Hordes of people huddled before the gate, relatives of the detainees, who asked me how Mr. or Mrs. so-and-so was faring.

The bus that had brought me to Haifa stopped at King George Street. I stood on a traffic island in the middle of the road, and an Arab boy tried to grab my suitcase and make a few pennies as a porter. I gripped my suitcase determinedly while also shaking off a Jewish predator who probably preyed on new immigrant girls and offered his room for the night.

As I stood there, the sun suddenly came out from behind the clouds and filled the street with its light. I took a deep breath and a wild joy seized me.

I was free.

I was nineteen.

I had my whole life ahead of me.

Ruth and her husband David ('Dadi') Uzrad, in the Lehavot Habashan fields, 1950. David appears to be in his working clothes after a long day of work and is holding their son, Yossi, on his shoulders.

AFTERWORD

– YOSSI UZRAD, 2026

In the early 1990s, decades after the end of World War II, my mother chose to break the wall of silence. My father traveled to a nearby town and, with their modest savings, bought a home computer.

For nearly two years, they sat side by side each evening for a few hours. My mother told her story in Hebrew, at a measured, dictated pace and my father listened, typing the words into the computer with two fingers.

The book came as a surprise to me. My mother and father never told me about their childhood in Berlin. Suddenly, I came to know Renée, a resistance fighter. A different woman, so unlike the mother I had known.

What made my mother begin telling the story of what she had endured during the Holocaust?

Many of the members of the kibbutz where I grew up were Holocaust survivors. In Israel's early years, the attitude toward survivors often bordered on contempt. "The Jews went like sheep to the slaughter" was a common phrase laden with criticism that they had not taken up arms and fought the Nazis. We, the second generation, did not ask. Life in the kibbutz was full of sunlight, nature, and a rich social world. The first to ask were her grandchildren. They wanted to know about her childhood in Germany.

My father chose to remain silent. There was no point, he did not believe, in reopening old wounds. That was probably the reason. He never told us, his sons, anything about the family he had lost.

My mother understood that the time had come to speak. If we did not preserve what had happened, who would believe that such a terrible war had taken place in the heart of civilization? That is how the book was born.

When I first read my mother's story, I was captivated, since most of the details were unknown to me. But at the time, I was consumed by my career and by raising a family and did not give it much attention. By the second reading, I was intrigued. The somewhat distant tone did not seem to match the character of *my* mother, who was energetic, outspoken, and deeply warm to everyone around her—a compassionate nurse in the fullest sense of the word. I began to think more about who she was then, and what made her write the book in that way. A sense of necessity, rather than pride, is what seemed to drive her.

Her youthful image as a resistance fighter, risking her life, seemed worlds away from the maternal figure I knew: embracing, protective, and endlessly devoted to her children. In the kibbutz, a small community of some two hundred families, the book was received with astonishment. Others had written books about their years in the camps. Those were different books: stories of prisoners and survival in the camps.

My mother's book was, on the surface, not a Holocaust book. It was the coming-of-age story of a young girl during wartime. The book opened many doors for her. She was invited to lecture and spoke in schools across Israel. Articles were written in newspapers, and several television features were produced, including one on the national broadcaster.

My mother joined student journeys to the extermination camps in Poland as a living witness. Because of the book, she was invited to "Yad Vashem" institute, where together with her friends she organized an annual ceremony honoring members of the Jewish French Résistance. She even received a certificate of appreciation at a special ceremony after her death. Without a doubt, the book changed her world. She had once been inward and closed. Afterwards, she opened herself to others. And in her final years, she was surrounded by the love of friends and family, who stayed by her side until her very last moments.

They Called Me Renée is an extraordinary story of a young girl coming of age during war and finding her purpose.

Undated. Ruth is third from the right.

Ruth

Ruth and her son, Yossi, in 1949.

Ruth Uzrad in later life.

Ruth and her husband, David.

Ruth; her mother, Berta Shiutz; her husband, David;
and her son, Yossi, at Kibbutz Lehavot HaBashan in 1949.

Ruth, David, and their son, Yossi, at the Kibbutz in 1950.

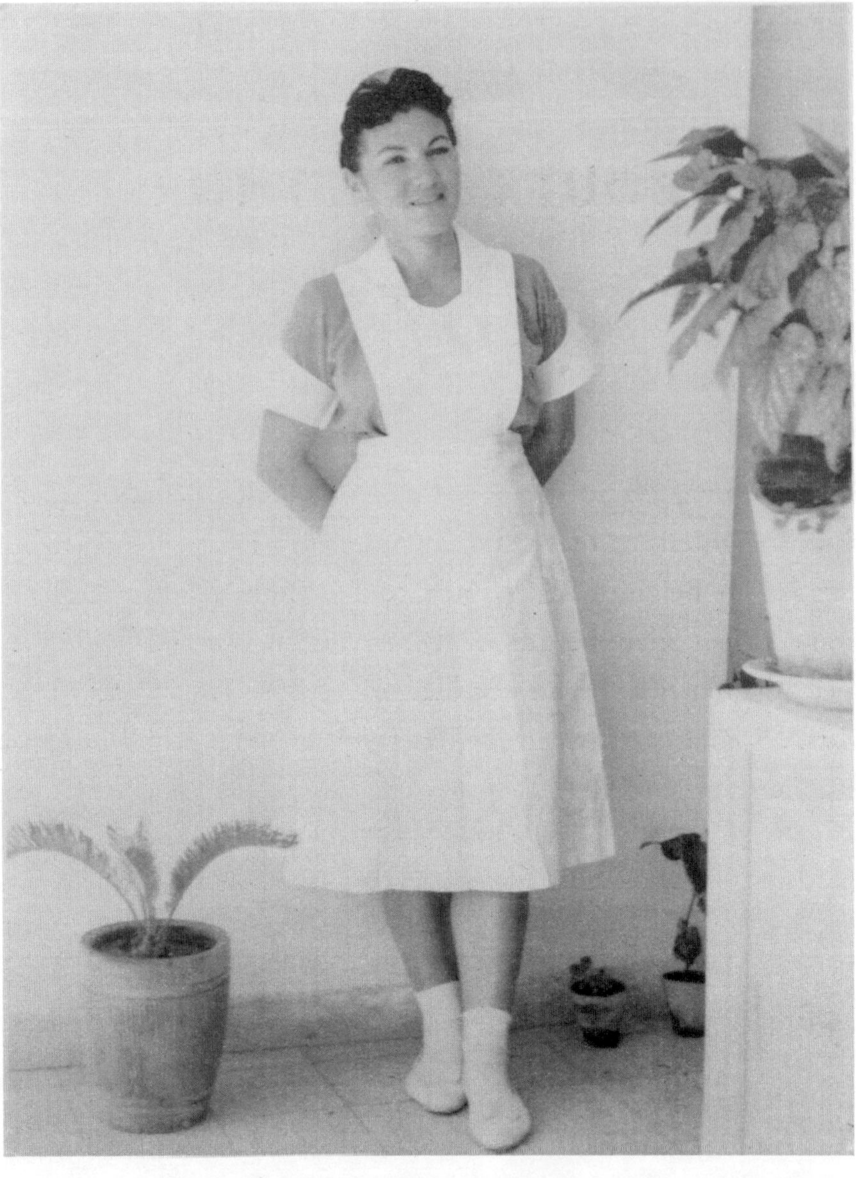

Ruth Uzrad in her nurse's uniform while studying to become a registered nurse at Beilinson Hospital in Petah Tikva, around 1960.

ABOUT THE AUTHOR

Ruth (Schutz) Uzrad was born in Berlin in 1925, the eldest of three daughters, to a religious Jewish family. During WWII she escaped to Belgium and continued her flight to the south of France, then Spain before finally arriving in Israel in 1945. She met and married David and had four sons, Yosef (known as Yossi), Raanan and twins, Ohad and Hovav. She passed away in 2015 at the age of 90.

RAISING READERS
Books Build Bright Futures

Dear Reader,

We'd love your attention for one more page to tell you about the crisis in children's reading, and what we can all do.

Studies have shown that reading for fun is the single biggest predictor of a child's future life chances – more than family circumstance, parents' educational background or income. It improves academic results, mental health, wealth, communication skills, ambition and happiness.[1]

The number of children reading for fun is in rapid decline. Young people have a lot of competition for their time. In 2024, 1 in 10 children and young people in the UK aged 5 to 18 did not own a single book at home.[2]

Hachette works extensively with schools, libraries and literacy charities, but here are some ways we can all raise more readers:

- Reading to children for just 10 minutes a day makes a difference
- Don't give up if children aren't regular readers – there will be books for them!
- Visit bookshops and libraries to get recommendations
- Encourage them to listen to audiobooks
- Support school libraries
- Give books as gifts

There's a lot more information about how to encourage children to read on our website: www.RaisingReaders.co.uk

Thank you for reading.

hachette LIVRE

---

[1] OECD. 2021. 21st-century readers: developing literacy skills in a digital world. Paris, France: OECD Publishing. https://www.oecd.org/en/publications/21st-century-readers_a83d84cb-en.html

[2] National Literacy Trust, Book Ownership in 2024, November 2024 https://nlt.cdn.ngo/media/documents/Book_ownership_in_2024